T0380806

THE
SERMON
ON THE
MOUNT

A PRACTICAL STUDY OF KINGDOM LIVING

HOLLY LAZZARO
FOREWORD BY MARCOS ORTEGA

WESTBOW
PRESS®
A DIVISION OF THOMAS NELSON
& ZONDERVAN

This book is a work of non-fiction. Unless otherwise noted, the author and the publisher make no explicit guarantees as to the accuracy of the information contained in this book and in some cases, names of people and places have been altered to protect their privacy.

WestBow Press books may be ordered through booksellers or by contacting:

WestBow Press
A Division of Thomas Nelson & Zondervan
1663 Liberty Drive
Bloomington, IN 47403
www.westbowpress.com
844-714-3454

Because of the dynamic nature of the Internet, any web addresses or links contained in this book may have changed since publication and may no longer be valid. The views expressed in this work are solely those of the author and do not necessarily reflect the views of the publisher, and the publisher hereby disclaims any responsibility for them.

Any people depicted in stock imagery provided by Getty Images are models, and such images are being used for illustrative purposes only. Certain stock imagery © Getty Images.

Unless otherwise indicated, all Scripture quotations are from the ESV® Bible (The Holy Bible, English Standard Version®), copyright © 2001 by Crossway, a publishing ministry of Good News Publishers. Used by permission. All rights reserved.

ISBN: 979-8-3850-0480-5 (sc)
ISBN: 979-8-3850-0481-2 (e)

Library of Congress Control Number: 2023915302

Print information available on the last page.

WestBow Press rev. date: 03/21/2024

CONTENTS

FOREWORD

When Holly first asked me to write the foreword to her new book on the Sermon on the Mount, I was standing in the center of Yellowstone National Park. My family and I were getting ready for a day of exploration and discovery. Beautiful fields of flowers. Majestic buffalo roaming through wide expanses. Thrilling waterfalls. Wolves lurking among the forests and bears fishing in streams.

But before we could explore, we needed to know where to look. And we needed a tool to help us see the beauty hidden throughout the park. My eight-year-old knew exactly what we needed: binoculars. We'd forgotten to bring a pair, and she spied ones just her size in the Old Faithful gift shop. They were our companion for the rest of our adventure, and she delighted in noting all the little things she would have missed if not for that handy little device. As I helped my daughter peer through her binoculars to get a better look at God's creation, I wondered to myself: How would Jesus have used these moments to teach his people about the Kingdom life?

Jesus was a master teacher and storyteller. He used parables to illustrate righteousness and questions to reveal hypocrisy. But he was not a professor that set himself up in a classroom or lecture hall. He was a rabbi who taught his followers as they traveled throughout the Judean countryside, never missing an opportunity to reveal the Kingdom to his disciples as he walked from village to village.

That's what makes the Sermon so unique. Rare are the extended accounts of these "on the way" teaching moments. The setting is not a synagogue or home, but a field on the side of a small mountain overlooking the Sea of Galilee. Surrounded by flowers and with birds singing in the background, Jesus delivered a sermon that now comprises one of the most important sections of wisdom literature in the entire New Testament.

Few portions of Scripture have garnered the attention given to the Sermon on the Mount. In fact, the sheer volume of theological, ethical, and even critical reflection on these three chapters has led historian Jaroslav Pelikan to surmise that writing "a history of the interpretation of the Sermon on the Mount throughout the past two millennia would virtually amount to an introduction to the entire development of Christian theology and ethics" (Pelikan, 1988, p. 229).

So why do we need another book? Why add to the ever-expanding library of books about the Sermon? Perhaps because even with all the analyses available to us, the Sermon remains—as the great John Stott once noted—one of "the least understood, and certainly...the least obeyed" portions of the entire New Testament. (Stott, 1987)

But why this book? Because of its unique perspective, format, and timeliness.

Perspective. Holly Lazzaro has been writing Bible studies since before her ministry, Study with Friends, began in 2014. And while her exegetical insights and eye for application could rival that of most preachers, she writes as a laywoman. A voice from the pews writing for those in the pews who are trying to figure out how Christianity is lived out in everyday ways. In an age of biblical illiteracy, there may be no more important perspective to learn from than one that prods the reader with the simple exhortation that sparked the Protestant Reformation: You can understand the Bible too! Dive in!

Format. When this sermon first came from the lips of Jesus, it was spoken to a group of disciples. Surely the revolutionary teachings sparked conversation and debate among the twelve, not to mention the crowd who was listening in. So what better way to study the sermon than in a small group or Bible study setting? The discussion questions and practical application will move you to sit down with someone else in your church—or with that unbelieving neighbor who lives on your block—and wrestle together with the difficult things Jesus expects of his Followers.

Timeliness. How are we to live as Christians—kingdom citizens and followers of King Jesus—in the chaos of today? When nations wage war against nations, ethnic hatred stubbornly persists, and suffering seems to spread to every corner of the globe, what does it mean to walk faithfully with Jesus? How do we develop a way of living, loving, thinking, and being that belongs to the other-worldly culture we call the Kingdom of God? These are pressing questions, and the following study charts a course that helps you love God and your neighbor in our contentious world.

If you use this book well, you'll find it functions much like those Yellowstone binoculars. Holly has written a tool to be used to see the beauty hidden throughout the sermon. I pray that, as you use it, you'll notice new insights or wrestle with difficult phrases. But more than that, I pray that you'll be captivated by the beauty of Jesus and the life he lays out in these three chapters. I pray that you'll fall in love with this familiar section of Scripture all over again and be inspired to follow Jesus into a Kingdom life that changes everything.

Rev. Marcos Ortega, July 2023

ACKNOWLEDGEMENTS

Thank you, Jesus, for giving me your Spirit in such a generous measure throughout my whole life and especially through the times we met in this text. Thank you for the Sermon.

Thank you to my family for supporting the expenditure of my time and energy to make the ministry of the Word something I can regularly do.

Thank you to Reverend Marcos Ortega, who has been a brother and sounding board for theological discussions and debates, and who read and challenged every word of this study to help me improve it. Thank you to Reverend Luke Mason, who has been a mentor and friend and who undoubtedly used too much toner printing this out to provide me with notes in the margins. Thank you to Reverend Matt Blazer, who has a special gift of encouragement that I needed for this project. Thank you to the Reverends Michael Davis, Tim Chiarot, Joe Kim, and John Dorr, who are wiser than I, and with their wisdom, helped me stay on the right path with the work in this study. Thank you to Gianna Lazzaro, Nancy Lesko, Marilyn Franzi, and Holly Grant for proofreading and catching the minutiae that would have driven us crazy had any of it been missed.

Many thanks to you, reader, for trusting me to shepherd you through this precious segment of scripture.

-Holly

WELCOME

Welcome to this eight-week study of the Sermon on the Mount. As with all Bible studies, two rules apply. First, a prayerful approach is the best. God will reveal what you need to understand: no more, no less. Your prayerful attitude is critical to receiving that revelation. Second, what you put into it will impact what you get from it. At Study With Friends, we provide several options for how you can take in the teaching (print, video, audio). You can decide how much time you spend on each day/week of study, but giving more time will yield a greater understanding of the content.

Each day of study includes partnering digital content. **Our video content is available <u>for free</u> on our YouTube channel: youtube.com/@study-with-friends**. However, if you are blessed by this or any of our studies, please prayerfully consider a donation of any amount. A monthly commitment is incredibly beneficial and allows us to budget for big projects like this. You can donate to our work at **studywithfriends.org/donate**. No amount is too small.

Scan the code to be directed to the Sermon on the Mount YouTube video playlist. Week one, day one is episode 1.1, week one, day two is episode 1.2, and so on. Look for this visual cue at the end of each day's study, and incorporate the video series into your homework time to broaden your understanding of the passage:

If you prefer an audio-only podcast, you can find us on **<u>all your favorite podcast services</u>**: Spotify, iTunes, Alexa (the command: "Alexa, play the Study With Friends podcast" will automatically pull up that week's episode), etc. Here is a quick code for you to connect with us on Spotify to listen to the podcast:

We have even developed a worship music playlist on Spotify for your meditations as you study the Sermon on the Mount:

You can stream the podcast from our website, studywithfriends.org. For the content of this study, search 'Sermon on the Mount' on the home page.

A NOTE FOR GROUP LEADERS

Any of the reflection questions can be used to facilitate your weekly group discussion. Be open to allowing the group (and the Holy Spirit) to select which questions you should explore together, but come to your weekly group prepared with a plan of what to cover. We suggest 1-3 questions on the biblical text and 1-3 on personal application from each week. Remember to stay in touch with your participants throughout the week to help with questions not addressed during group time. Strongly encourage your participants to utilize the digital content available and be sure to engage with it yourself as it contains additional teaching and insight.

As a facilitator rather than a teacher, permit yourself to learn alongside your group. You won't always have answers to your group's questions. The digital teaching/discussion should provide more insight, and you can reach out to us at Study With Friends (info@studywithfriends.org) if you have lingering questions. Interacting with you about the Bible is our favorite thing; we *love* supporting group facilitators like you!

All scripture references are quoted from the ESV Bible translation unless otherwise indicated.

WEEK ONE

INTRODUCTION
(MATTHEW 5:1-2)

Seeing the crowds, he went up on the mountain, and when he sat down,
His disciples came to Him. [2] And he opened His
mouth and taught them, saying:
–Matthew 5:1-2

The Sermon on the Mount is Jesus' description of the Christian life.

While the term Christian would come much later, Jesus utters the directions here to guide us in living the life He desires for us. In each section of the Sermon, He clarifies His intentions by contrasting Christian and non-Christian ideals.

While crowds may have overheard what Jesus taught in this sermon, He directed this teaching toward those already following him. This is an important starting point. The Sermon on the Mount is not a self-improvement plan for everyone, but a standard for those already committed to Him. The principles outlined in these chapters of the Bible apply to all areas of our lives.

The Sermon on the Mount is a complete and comprehensive description of the Christian life. In it, Jesus describes how to be His disciple in full view of the Law and teachings that came before Him. The Sermon is a call to follow Jesus' teachings and live a life characterized by love, humility, and obedience to God's commands.

DAY ONE

THE SERMON AND THE OLD TESTAMENT

Just as Moses received the Law at Mount Sinai, Jesus went to a mountainside to teach His disciples. He may have done this to draw a parallel between his words in the Sermon and the Law given by Moses. Even the words in verses 5:1-2, "he went up on the mountain" are reminiscent of Exodus 19:3 when Moses did the same. Within these verses, parallels between Jesus and Moses are abundant. For example, there were twelve tribes in Israel who were charged with upholding and living out the law – there were also twelve apostles of Jesus who were charged with making disciples in a new Israel. In both cases, commandments were given and obedience was expected.

What are some other parallels you can think of between Jesus and Moses?

_____

_____

Why do you think that understanding the similarities between Jesus and Moses might be important in the whole context of scripture?

_____

_____

The parallels between Moses and Jesus are no accident. The status that Moses held in the Israelite community was immense. There could be only one that would exceed that status, and that was God Himself. Enter Jesus, who fulfilled the promises and prophecies in Israel. The covenants made with Moses, David, and others all pointed to a coming Messiah: a prophet, priest, and king.

At the time Jesus gave the Sermon, those who understood Jewish scriptures would have been expecting a new Moses based on many Old Testament scriptures, but we will focus only on two: Deuteronomy 18:15 and Isaiah 43:15-19. First, read the Deuteronomy verse:

> *The LORD your God will raise up for you a prophet like me from among you, from your brothers—it is to him you shall listen.*

This is an easy passage to use for developing the Jesus/Moses precept. While Joshua was the initial fulfillment of this passage, there is a second, greater fulfillment in Jesus.

What are some examples of Old Testament prophets?

_____

_____

What is your understanding of the role of a prophet?

_____

_____

How did Jesus fulfill the expectation of the prophet from this verse?

_____

_____

Another reason the Israelites would be looking for a new Moses comes from Isaiah 43:15-19:

> *15I am the LORD, your Holy One, the Creator of Israel, your King." 16Thus says the LORD, who makes a way in the sea, a path in the mighty waters, 17 who brings forth chariot and horse, army and warrior; they lie down, they cannot rise, they are extinguished, quenched like a wick: 18"Remember not the former things, nor consider the things of old. 19Behold, I am doing a new thing; now it springs forth, do you not perceive it? I will make a way in the wilderness and rivers in the desert.*

This passage does not mention Moses by name. Circle the places you see references to Moses' leadership in this passage.

2

Do you see any connection between the miracles cited here and the coming miracles of Christ and His kingdom? Explain.

_____

_____

There are two reasons that these Old Testament passages (and many others) help us better frame The Sermon and our understanding of it. First, studying scripture in the context of the audience who first heard it is always useful. Second, these passages remind us of God's great plan and how He fulfilled it in Christ. We must understand this fulfillment as we read on and learn from Jesus. Before He can teach us, we must believe He has the authority to do so. He is the Greater Moses, God Himself in the flesh. What better Teacher could there be?

Watch Study With Friends Video Series: The Sermon, Episode 1.1

DAY TWO

THE SERMON AND THE NEW TESTAMENT

The Sermon on the Mount provides us with a discipleship perspective that is reiterated in the writings of Peter, Paul, and the entire New Testament. That should be no surprise because scripture is cohesive and consistent. However, The Sermon on the Mount might especially remind you of the Book of James.

Both texts represent Jesus' words in different but essential ways. Some even believe that the book of James is a commentary on the Sermon. At the very least, the Sermon and the Book of James share a common theme: practical Christianity. They both remind us that "the ultimate purpose of Christian instruction, the goal of doctrine, is a godly character and righteous behavior… [G]enuine faith is more than a matter of simply acknowledging the right concepts; it is right living in accordance with those concepts" (McCartney, 2009, p. 3).

If you have ever heard the expression 'scripture teaches scripture' (or even if you haven't), settle in with that concept for today's study assignment. There is not much other instruction in this study segment because we can rest confidently in how the book of James comments on, elaborates on, and supports understanding of the Sermon.

See Appendix A for a more comprehensive list of the shared themes in James and the Sermon. As we start our study, we will choose only a few related texts to emphasize the Sermon's overarching themes. After each set of scriptures, reflect on how reading them together helps you understand each one better.

Mercy:

Blessed are the merciful, for they shall receive mercy. (Matthew 5:7)

. . .judgment is without mercy to one who has shown no mercy. Mercy triumphs over judgment. (James 2:13)

Peace:

Blessed are the peacemakers, for they shall be called sons of God. (Matthew 5:9)

And a harvest of righteousness is sown in peace by those who make peace. (James 3:18)

_____

_____

Trials:

[10] Blessed are those who are persecuted for righteousness' sake, for theirs is the kingdom of heaven. [11] Blessed are you when others revile you and persecute you and utter all kinds of evil against you falsely on my account. [12] Rejoice and be glad, for your reward is great in heaven, for so they persecuted the prophets who were before you. (Matthew 5:10–12)

Count it all joy, my brothers, when you meet trials of various kinds. (James 1:2)

_____

_____

The necessity of righteousness:

. . . I tell you, unless your righteousness exceeds that of the scribes and Pharisees, you will never enter the kingdom of heaven. (Matthew 5:20)

. . . whoever keeps the whole law but fails in one point has become accountable for all of it. (James 2:10)

_____

_____

Treasures:

Do not lay up for yourselves treasures on earth, where moth and rust destroy and where thieves break in and steal. (Matthew 6:19)

[2]Your riches have rotted and your garments are moth-eaten. [3]Your gold and silver have corroded, and their corrosion will be evidence against you and will eat your flesh like fire. You have laid up treasure in the last days. [4]Behold, the wages of the laborers who mowed your fields, which you kept back by fraud, are crying out against you, and the cries of the harvesters have reached the ears of the Lord of hosts. [5]You have lived on the earth in luxury and in self-indulgence. You have fattened your hearts in a day of slaughter. (James 5:2-5)

_____

_____

God's provision:

Therefore do not be anxious about tomorrow, for tomorrow will be anxious for itself. Sufficient for the day is its own trouble. (Matthew 6:34)

[13]Come now, you who say, "Today or tomorrow we will go into such and such a town and spend a year there and trade and make a profit"—[14]yet you do not know what tomorrow will bring. What is your life? For you are a mist that appears for a little time and then vanishes. (James 4:13-14)

_____

_____

Be slow to judge:

[1]Judge not, that you be not judged. [2]For with the judgment you pronounce you will be judged, and with the measure you use it will be measured to you. [3]Why do you see the speck that is in your brother's eye, but do not notice the log that is in your own eye? [4]Or how can you say to your brother, "Let me take the speck out of your eye," when there is the log in your own eye? [5]You hypocrite, first take the log out of your own eye, and then you will see clearly to take the speck out of your brother's eye. (Matthew 7:1-5)

[11]Do not speak evil against one another, brothers. The one who speaks against a brother or judges his brother, speaks evil against the law and judges the law. But if you judge the law, you are not a

doer of the law but a judge. ¹²There is only one lawgiver and judge, he who is able to save and to destroy. But who are you to judge your neighbor? (James 4:11-12)

_____

_____

Ask and receive:

⁷Ask, and it will be given to you; seek, and you will find; knock, and it will be opened to you. ⁸For everyone who asks receives, and the one who seeks finds, and to the one who knocks it will be opened. (Matthew 7:7-8)

²You desire and do not have, so you murder. You covet and cannot obtain, so you fight and quarrel. You do not have, because you do not ask. ³You ask and do not receive, because you ask wrongly, to spend it on your passions. (James 4:2-3)

_____

_____

Put words into action:

²⁴ Everyone then who hears these words of mine and does them will be like a wise man who built his house on the rock. ²⁵And the rain fell, and the floods came, and the winds blew and beat on that house, but it did not fall, because it had been founded on the rock. ²⁶And everyone who hears these words of mine and does not do them will be like a foolish man who built his house on the sand. ²⁷And the rain fell, and the floods came, and the winds blew and beat against that house, and it fell, and great was the fall of it. (Matthew 7:24-27)

. . . be doers of the word, and not hearers only, deceiving yourselves. (James 1:22)

_____

_____

Does the comparison between the Sermon and James help you better grasp these scripture passages in practical ways? If so, how?

_____

_____

The Sermon stands tall across the entire New Testament. The teachings in each of the New Testament books reflect, in some way, most of the content of the Sermon. As such, whether you are a new believer or a mature Christian, the Sermon has something to say to all of us. In each study week, we will examine more Old and New Testament passages that help enlighten the Sermon (and vice versa!).

Watch Study With Friends Video Series: The Sermon, Episode 1.2

DAY THREE

THE USEFULNESS OF THE SERMON

Are the standards that Jesus describes here practical? And if so, how do we live the kind of life Jesus depicts, in full view of grace, without becoming legalistic law-abiders like some of the Pharisees? Are these three chapters of scripture relevant to our modern lives or merely moral and ethical ideals to keep in mind?

The Sermon on the Mount is not metaphorical. Don't read this passage as poetry or symbolism. Don't keep it at a distance. The Sermon on the Mount wakes us from complacency and brings us into a more intimate relationship with our Savior. It was intentionally counter-cultural when it was spoken and remains so today. It can do mighty work in us if we allow it.

What portions of the Sermon seem impractical or irrelevant to you and why?

_____

_____

Jesus is merciful in His clarity when describing His followers in this passage. As we study together, it will be vital for us to remember the balance between sanctification and justification. As John Stott (2020) describes, "the standards of the Sermon are neither readily attainable by everyone, nor totally unattainable by anyone. To put them beyond anybody's reach is to ignore the purpose of Christ's sermon; to put them within everybody's is to ignore the reality of human sin. They are attainable alright, but only by those who have experienced the new birth in Christ."

In each line of the Sermon, Jesus expands on a small piece of verse 6:8: ***Do not be like them***. In these five words, Jesus emphasizes the importance of kingdom living according to the "do" behaviors and attitudes that He expands upon throughout. These five words sum up the Sermon, so let's write them down and memorize them now.

Write the five words, in all capitals, that sum up the entire Sermon:

_____

The Sermon calls Christians to live in a way that is counter to the values and beliefs of the culture around them. Jesus teaches principles and practices that are fundamentally different from those of the world, and He challenges His followers to live out these teachings in their daily lives.

One way in which the Sermon calls us to be counter-cultural is by emphasizing the importance of inner righteousness vs. outward hypocrisy. Jesus teaches that true righteousness is not simply a matter of outwardly following a set of rules or laws but a matter of the heart. He emphasizes the importance of humility, meekness, and peacemaking, which are often seen as weaknesses in a culture that values power and dominance.

Another way in which the Sermon calls us to be counter-cultural is by teaching the importance of love. Jesus teaches that love is the foundation of God's commands and that true love is characterized by a willingness to forgive others and do good to those who harm us. This kind of love goes against the grain of a culture that often values personal revenge and retaliation.

Jesus reminds His disciples "Do not be like them" by teaching that prayer, fasting, and material possessions should be used in the service of God's kingdom rather than for personal gain or to gain recognition. Jesus teaches that these practices should be done in secret rather than being done for the sake of being seen by others, which goes against the cultural norm of showing off and seeking fame.

How do the qualities of a Christian prescribed by Jesus in the Sermon differ from how the world sees Christians?

_____

_____

The Sermon calls Christians to live in a way that contradicts the culture around us. Jesus teaches principles and practices that are fundamentally different from those of the world and challenges his followers to live out these teachings in their daily lives, emphasizing the importance of inner righteousness, love, humility, meekness, and putting God's kingdom first in our prayer, fasting, and material possessions. This way of life calls for Christians to go against cultural norms and values and live a truly different life from the world.

Scan the Sermon and find as many ways as you can where Jesus calls His disciples to be counter-cultural:

John Stott (2020) calls the Sermon "the nearest thing to a manifesto that [Jesus] ever uttered, for it is his own description of what he wanted his followers to be and do."

The question of the usefulness of the Sermon lies fully in our own hands.

Watch Study With Friends Video Series: The Sermon, Episode 1.3

The Sermon
VIDEO SERIES

DAY FOUR

THE AUTHENTICITY OF THE SERMON

Before we dive into the Sermon, there is an important question to address: Did Jesus really teach this? While some of us might simply take this for granted, others may be curious about the imagery of the single, sweeping Sermon pictured in Matthew versus the other gospels' portrayal of these teachings in different settings. Our response to the Sermon will naturally be rooted in our confidence in its authenticity, so let's explore that a bit.

First, a global understanding of the synergy between the gospels is helpful. They are sometimes portrayed as four different versions of the same story, and there is truth to that. However, each was written to a specific audience for a specific reason.

There are more similarities in the content of Matthew, Mark, and Luke than in the gospel of John, which is why these three books are often called the 'synoptic gospels.' The biggest differences are in the perspective and purpose of these three books. Matthew presents Jesus as the fulfillment of the Old Testament scriptures. In Mark, Jesus' miracle-working power is set beside His suffering and death to help us understand Him better. Luke, writing to a different audience, points out how God's salvation promise includes all people over all time.[1]

Each gospel, then, presents a different facet of the same Jesus. To understand any differences in the gospel portrayals, we should first ask: What was the purpose of this text? Let's think of it in an everyday setting. If I told you a true story of my trip to the grocery store, I might tell it two ways. First, I could tell it like this:

> I went to the store yesterday very early in the evening. It was just after dusk, but the parking lot lights were on, so I could see most of the parking lot very well. I parked my car towards the edge of the parking lot, close to some trees. As I walked into the store, a coyote came out of the woods and crossed my path. We both stopped dead in our tracks. I had no idea what to do. Eventually, the

---

[1] Study With Friends has more in-depth studies on all three of the synoptic gospels. For more on their themes, please refer to those studies which can be downloaded for free at studywithfriends.org.

coyote moved on, and I went into the store. I did my shopping, but it took a bit longer than I anticipated because there was a great sale on canned goods, so I stocked up. After shopping, I sure was careful to look around for that coyote before I exited the store's safety!

Or I could tell it like this:

I went to the grocery store last night. On my way into the store, I saw a coyote. That was crazy. But you would not believe the sale they had on canned goods. I guess they do this yearly sale, but I didn't remember that. I had no intention of buying as many canned goods as I left with, but I could not resist the savings! I had to make room in my pantry for all the cans I bought; some are still in my garage. You should head over there before the sale ends.

Can both stories be 100% true?

_____

_____

Can these two accounts be about the same person, at the same time, having the same experience?

_____

_____

Summarize the purpose of each account.

_____

_____

How does the purpose of the story influence how the account is told?

_____

_____

I shared one experience in two different ways, and both were 100% true. But my purpose for telling the story resulted in a different emphasis.

This is a good way to consider the differences in the gospels and the differences in the ways the teachings of the Sermon are portrayed. Is it possible the discourse was given all at once? Yes. Is it possible it was on a mountain? Sure. Matthew and Luke present this as an actual sermon given by Jesus, give it precise geographical context, and ascribe it to His early ministry in Galilee. But this does not mean the Sermon is a word-for-word transcription of a specific experience, especially since both authors wrote in Greek and Jesus spoke Aramaic. There are differences in the versions, but the core teaching is the same: Jesus' instruction on practical Christianity.

Some suggest we might even understand these teachings as having occurred over a period of time for the disciples as a sort of summer school before they are dispatched to the work of spreading the gospel. That's a summer school I'd like to attend!

Aside from the global understanding of how the gospels weave together, another argument for the authenticity of the Sermon on the Mount is the fact that it is found in *this* gospel: Matthew. The gospel of Matthew was written for a Jewish-Christian audience, which means Matthew would have had a strong motivation to record the Sermon accurately, as it reframed some Jewish teachings of the time.

Topics such as inner righteousness, love for enemies, and humility are more deeply understood because of how Jesus describes them in the Sermon. This reframing might have been hard to swallow for early Jewish Christians, underscoring the authenticity. If it was unpopular, but still included in Matthew's gospel, it is more likely to be authentic.

Compare Exodus 21:23-25 to Matthew 5:38-42:

_____

_____

Considering the above apparent contrast between the Torah and the Sermon, write Matthew 5:17 here:

_____

_____

Jesus came to clarify and culminate God's will.

On day two of this week, we examined the Sermon in the context of the New Testament, mostly in the book of James. Because the Sermon contains teachings that are consistent with other teachings of Jesus found in the gospels and the writings of the New Testament authors, this is also an argument for the Sermon's authenticity. Each week we will dive deeper into those cross references.

The Sermon is rooted in the Jewish tradition and reflects the Jewish context in which Jesus lived and taught. The Sermon contains many references to the Hebrew Bible, and the teachings of Jesus are often presented as a commentary on the Hebrew Bible. This suggests that the Sermon is rooted in the Jewish tradition and reflects the Jewish context in which Jesus lived and taught.

List as many Old Testament references as you can find in the Sermon:

_____

_____

It is evident from the writings of the early Church Fathers that the Sermon had a significant impact on the early Christian community and was considered an important part of Jesus' teachings. Elliot Nesch (2018) says, "[w]hat the lost and dying world needs today is not a new definition of Christianity, but a present-day demonstration of Christianity. Rather than redefine Christianity to accommodate our present generation, we must re-discover Christianity from the apostolic generation. In this regard, the early Christian writings may be a helpful tool in order to get us closer to that apostolic era of doctrine and practice." Nesch cites writings by "those disciples of Christ, also known as the Apostolic Fathers and Ante-Nicene Fathers, who lived prior to the Council of Nicaea in AD 325." These very early writings reference the Sermon, again underpinning the text's authenticity.

How does the Sermon's impact on the early church help you embrace the authenticity of the text?

_____

_____

The Sermon is found in one of the most historically accurate gospels, contains teachings that are unique *to* Jesus and are consistent with other teachings *about* Jesus, is rooted in the Jewish tradition, and was influential in the early Christian community. Let's accept these authentic teachings of Christ as influential in our lives too.

Watch Study With Friends Video Series: The Sermon, Episode 1.4

DAY FIVE

OUR RESPONSE TO THE SERMON

Dietrich Bonhoeffer, a German theologian and pastor during World War II, developed the concept of "cheap grace" in his book *The Cost of Discipleship* (Bonhoeffer, 1979/1937). He argued that the grace of God is often wrongly reduced to a cheap and superficial understanding in which individuals can continue to live in sin and still be forgiven by God. According to Bonhoeffer, this "cheap grace" is a denial of the cost of following Jesus and the demand for repentance and obedience.

In the Sermon, Jesus teaches the disciples about the true nature of the kingdom of God and the demands of being a disciple. He calls for repentance, righteousness, and obedience to God's commands. For example, in verse 5:20, Jesus says, "For I tell you unless your righteousness exceeds that of the scribes and Pharisees, you will never enter the kingdom of heaven." This statement highlights the fact that mere outward adherence to religious rules and regulations is not enough to enter the kingdom of God. True righteousness comes from a deep internal transformation, genuine repentance, and obedience to God.

Bonhoeffer's concept of cheap grace helps us understand and respond to the Sermon because it rejects a superficial understanding of God's grace. He argues that grace is not a license to sin but the power to overcome sin and live a life of obedience and righteousness.

Write your own definition of the word 'cheap.'

_____

_____

The Sermon also emphasizes the importance of living a life of love and compassion for others. Jesus teaches the importance of loving our enemies and turning the other cheek instead of seeking revenge. This message of love and compassion is what Bonhoeffer calls "costly grace," as it calls for a radical transformation of the self where individuals are willing to put the needs of others before their own. In *The Cost of Discipleship*, Bonhoeffer writes, "Cheap grace is the preaching of forgiveness without requiring repentance, baptism without church discipline, Communion without confession, absolution without personal confession. Cheap grace is grace without discipleship, grace without the Cross, grace without Jesus Christ, living and incarnate" (Bonhoeffer, 1979/1937, pp. 44-45).

How might 'grace without discipleship' be a negative thing in someone's life?

How might we consider our response to the Sermon to be 'costly?'

The Sermon on the Mount calls for a deeper understanding of the grace of God, which demands repentance, righteousness, and obedience. It emphasizes the importance of living a life of love and compassion for others. This response to grace is difficult (costly) but worth it, as through it, we experience a radical transformation of the self.

Another great thinker who helps us shape our response to the Sermon is Herman Bavinck, a Dutch Reformed theologian who believed that God's redemptive work, also known as grace, is how God restores the natural order of things. He believed that humanity's fall from grace in the Garden of Eden caused a disruption in the natural order, leading to the corruption of humanity and the natural world. However, through the work of Jesus Christ, God's grace restores the natural order and brings about the redemption of humanity and the natural world. (Veenhof/ Wolters, 2006.)

Bavinck believed that God's grace is not just a transaction but a transformative work that changes the very nature of humanity. This transformation begins with regeneration, in which God imparts new spiritual life to individuals, enabling them to have faith in Jesus Christ and be saved. This new spiritual life is not something added to an individual's natural life but rather a new mode of existence. It's a change in the innermost being of an individual, which results in a new way of thinking, feeling, and willing. This is what the Sermon is focused on: living the transformed life.

How does Bavink's concept of grace restoring all of nature impact your thoughts about yourself or your relationship with God?

_____

_____

How does this concept influence how you respond to the Sermon?

_____

_____

Herman Bavinck asserts that God's grace is not just transactional but a transformative work that changes the very nature of humanity and the natural world. The work of Jesus Christ enables us to respond rightly to our salvation. Through the process of regeneration, God imparts new spiritual life to us, giving us the power to make real, lasting changes in our lives and the lives of those around us. That is what the Sermon is all about.

Watch Study With Friends Video Series: The Sermon, Episode 1.5

WEEK TWO

KINGDOM CHARACTER
(MATTHEW 5:3-12)

*³Blessed are the poor in spirit, for theirs is the kingdom of heaven.
⁴Blessed are those who mourn, for they shall be comforted.
⁵Blessed are the meek, for they shall inherit the earth.
⁶Blessed are those who hunger and thirst for
righteousness, for they shall be satisfied.
⁷Blessed are the merciful, for they shall receive mercy.
⁸Blessed are the pure in heart, for they shall see God.
⁹Blessed are the peacemakers, for they shall be called sons of God.
¹⁰Blessed are those who are persecuted for righteousness'
sake, for theirs is the kingdom of heaven.
¹¹Blessed are you when others revile you and persecute you
and utter all kinds of evil against you falsely on my account.
¹²Rejoice and be glad, for your reward is great in heaven, for
so they persecuted the prophets who were before you.*
–Matthew 5:3-12

Jesus begins the Sermon on the Mount with a list, often called The Beatitudes. This set of blessings sets the tone for the Sermon.

For modern-day Christians, the Beatitudes provide a clear guide for how to live a life that is pleasing to God. They challenge us to be humble, compassionate, pure, and peacemaking even in the face of persecution. The Beatitudes are a reminder that true blessedness is not found in wealth, power, or status, but in a right relationship with God through faith in Jesus Christ.

This passage is a call to reflection: the Beatitudes provide an avenue for the Holy Spirit to search us and find wayward ways in us. It is a call for testimony to the world, to be a representation of Christ to all we meet.

DAY ONE

WHY START HERE?

Since we serve the God of order, we should pause and consider the Sermon's structure. We will get into some granular structural issues as we go along, but for now, let's ask ourselves: Why start this very important passage of scripture here?

What are your initial thoughts on this list being the start of the Sermon?

_____

_____

It is important to note that the Beatitudes are not a list of works that must be done to *earn* salvation or blessings. They describe the attitudes and dispositions of those who are *already* in a relationship with God through faith in Jesus Christ. The Beatitudes are not a checklist for spiritual growth but a call to live a life transformed by the presence and power of God.

What is the appeal of a spiritual checklist?

_____

_____

What is the danger of a spiritual checklist?

_____

_____

Read the list in Galatians 5:22–23. Compare and contrast this list with Matthew 5:3–12:

_____

_____

While not a checklist, Matthew 5:3-12 is still undeniably a list. As it is presented, this list is a great way to get the audience's attention. It forces us to look at ourselves deeply and immediately before we move on to the rest of the Sermon. We ask ourselves: if this is how a Christian is called to live, how do I fit in? Can I and should I be doing better?

When you look at this list, are there any immediate responses the Spirit places in you?

_____

_____

This list creates a Spirit-filled hunger in us. The repetition of the word "blessed" engages us in a desire to please God and be the people included in the blessing. Some of us may even try to pick one or two lines and really live into that characteristic, hoping that a blessing will result. If blessings are available, we want them! Others will closely identify with the description of poor, grieving, meek, or persecuted, and claim the blessings due.

Do any of the descriptions in the Beatitudes particularly resonate with you?

_____

_____

Are there any descriptions in the Beatitudes that convict you?

_____

_____

Jesus knew how to build a case. By starting the Sermon with this description of the blessed, He engages the audience of the time and the scripture-reading disciple today to lean in, pay attention, and take note.

Watch Study With Friends Video Series: The Sermon, Episode 2.1

DAY TWO

WHAT DOES BLESSED MEAN?

The meaning of "blessed" has three elements. First, it implies happiness and satisfaction. People who are "blessed" are flourishing and content because of their relationship with Jesus. This application has a right-now, real-life quality. Ernest Ligon calls the Beatitudes "the basic formula for mental health" (Ligon, 1935, p. 91). In other words: we should embrace these qualities for a good and happy life right now.

Secondly, these verses have two components: "Blessed are/for they shall (or theirs is)" This means the blessings also have an eschatological focus or future promise. These attributes are worthy of focusing on for our eternal future. In other words: embrace these qualities so that something good can happen for you in the future.

Choose two of the blessings and describe some ways these characteristics can have a right-now <u>and</u> a future focus in the Christian life:

_____

_____

_____

_____

Third, there is a theme of conditionality in play. God provides His perfect gift of salvation through Christ with unconditional love. We did nothing to deserve it, no work of ours accomplished it. It is completely unconditional. Christians call this *justification*.

But God also gives us guidance on how to live a life satisfying to Him and beneficial to us. A theological word for this is *sanctification*. God will always love us but He may not always be pleased with us. Whether He is pleased is conditional upon our understanding and embracing kingdom living. This precept of justification and sanctification/conditional and unconditional existing in the same space informs how we see God, scripture, and ourselves.

Jesus said in John 10:10 that He came so that we might have life and have it abundantly. Both here in the Sermon and there in the gospel of John, we see a distinction (but connection) between eternal life and the quality of our earthly life until then.

In the Old Testament, God made promises or covenants. Each of these covenants was also conditional and unconditional. In the Study With Friends Bible study *Understanding the Old Testament* (Lazzaro, 2021), we develop the juxtaposition of unconditional/conditional covenantal promises in much greater detail. Still, it's important to mention here that the Beatitudes reflect consistency in God's disposition towards us: He is unconditional in His love and desire to be in a relationship with us and conditional in His rewards and blessings for those who pursue His ways.

How do you feel about the balance of unconditionality and conditionality in our relationship with God?

_____

_____

Are there any examples in your life that help you to make sense of this juxtaposition?

_____

_____

There can be elements of unconditionality and conditionality in many kinds of relationships. For example, God often develops the idea of His covenantal disposition towards us with passages of scripture that use marriage as a parable. However, some find the parent/child relationship more helpful as they attempt to wrap their brains around this paradigm.

Ultimately, all human examples fall short of fully describing how God loves us. We are wise to form our best understanding of God's love not by looking at human relationships we may experience but by looking at how God has revealed Himself in scripture and through His Son. Even then, we can barely comprehend it.

Watch Study With Friends Video Series: The Sermon, Episode 2.2

DAY THREE

WHO IS BLESSED?

Because of how this section of scripture is presented and how it has been translated, there are different interpretations about who the blessed might be, particularly in verse 5:3. Much debate has occurred over whether the "poor" are spiritually or practically poor. We will look more deeply at that tomorrow.

When we examine who are the blessed, we must return to the core principle of the Sermon: these are Jesus' teachings for His disciples. Therefore, *we* are the Blessed; we who follow Him and love Him and accept His lordship over our lives. Remember, the condition for blessing does include radical obedience.

Reflect on your ownership of God's blessings and how that impacts you. Resist the temptation to think lofty thoughts here. Instead, take a beat to let the name Blessed fall on you fresh right now, and record your reflections.

_____

_____

Even with this in mind, it is easy to falsely separate this list into different types of Christians. However, this list is not about different types of Christians, it is describing the qualities of *all* Christians. As we read them, we must accept that these are not elite qualities, achievable only by the saintliest of Jesus' disciples; these attributes are the standard that Jesus expects every Christian to seek. Therefore, if Jesus commands that we embody these attributes, He will help us find and truly possess them.

The Holy Spirit works in us to produce all of these qualities for our good and God's glory: humble dependence on God (5:3); acute mourning and grief over our sinful state (5:4); gentle humility from an awareness of our own need for grace (5:5); hunger for spiritual not material wealth (5:6); compassion to the point of radical solidarity (5:7); inward morality, not just outward rule-keeping (5:8); pursuing peace by stepping into conflict (5:9); and those who are persecuted for embodying these qualities (5:10-12).

This list of qualities we should all possess, much like the Ten Commandments, focuses first on how we relate to God (the first four commandments and the first four Beatitudes) and then how we relate to each other (the last six commandments and the last four Beatitudes).

You may recall Jesus stressing this order of priorities when He boiled it all down for His disciples in Matthew 22:37-40, saying "[37]You shall love the Lord your God with all your heart and with all your soul and with all your mind. [38]This is the great and first commandment. [39]And a second is like it: You shall love your neighbor as yourself. [40]On these two commandments depend all the Law and the Prophets."

Reflect on the consistency of priorities in these passages:

_____

_____

Read Psalm 1 and reflect on the blessings in that passage. Does this Psalm deepen your understanding of the Beatitudes? Why or why not?

_____

_____

Isn't it comforting (and awe-inspiring) to see how consistent God is when He relates to us, instructs us, and comforts us?

This first portion of the Sermon powerfully illustrates the nature of the Christian life marked by humility, righteousness, peace, and faithfulness. The Beatitudes teach the importance of recognizing our spiritual poverty, how and why we must grieve over sin, seek righteousness, show mercy, make peace, and be prepared for persecution. These teachings are just as relevant today as they were when they were first spoken by Jesus, and they continue to be a source of guidance and inspiration for Christians worldwide.

Watch Study With Friends Video Series: The Sermon, Episode 2.3

DAY FOUR

THE BLESSINGS

We can understand the blessings better by putting them into a cautious but useful grouping of threes: verses 5:3-5, 5:6-8, and 5:9-11. Considering these are qualities of all Christians and not a list of different types of Christians, let's explore how we might understand and embrace these qualities better.

³Blessed are the poor in spirit, for theirs is the kingdom of heaven. ⁴Blessed are those who mourn, for they shall be comforted. ⁵Blessed are the meek, for they shall inherit the earth. –Matthew 5:3-5

Circle the descriptive words in the verses above. What do these people have in common?

_____

_____

We can look at these first three blessings as those given to those who are disadvantaged in some way. These are people who are economically impoverished or physically/emotionally oppressed. Grouping these first three blessings together helps us avoid the argument over what kind of "poor" person Jesus describes in verse 3. There has been much debate over whether Jesus was talking about spiritual poverty, as Matthew says, "poor in spirit," or economic poverty, as Luke seems to describe in the parallel passage (Luke 6:20), by simply saying "poor."

Simply being disadvantaged is not the formula for the blessing. These people recognize their need for God in both temporal and spiritual ways. They understand the importance of faithfulness amid any kind of oppression, and they embrace solidarity with other oppressed people. This group of blessings focuses on those who love and trust God and love others with actionable compassion and justice. James helps us understand these blessings even better by providing a portrait of the opposite.

Read James 2:1-13 and describe how James enlightens these first three blessings:

_____

_____

James provides further understanding in Chapter 4. Read James 4:9-10 and note how this passage deepens our understanding of the first three blessings:

_____

_____

The next three blessings focus on something different:

⁶ **"Blessed are those who hunger and thirst for righteousness, for they shall be satisfied. ⁷"Blessed are the merciful, for they shall receive mercy. ⁸"Blessed are the pure in heart, for they shall see God.** *-Matthew 5:6-8*

Circle the descriptive words in the verses above. What do these people have in common?

_____

_____

There is no question God commands righteousness and justice. These three blessings come directly after describing those who are oppressed or disadvantaged in some way. Coincidence? Not with a perfect God. If we read these three blessings as connected not just to each other but to those preceding, we have a bright and beautiful view of the type of Christian Jesus is calling us to be: one who is hungry for righteousness, one who is merciful to all, and one who is purely focused on these things for God's glory and not their own.

Righteousness, mercy, justice, and purity of heart are inextricably linked in the same way that faith and work are inextricably linked. By looking at these three blessings together, we can see that connection.

God commands righteousness, mercy, and purity of heart all over the bible, not just here in the Sermon. Each passage in the left column adds to our comprehension of righteousness, mercy, and purity of heart. Draw lines to the quality on the right where you see the connection:

James 2:13
Psalm 73:1
Proverbs 11:17   Righteousness
Micah 6:8
Colossians 3:12
Proverbs 21:3
1 Timothy 1:5   Mercy
Luke 6:36
1 John 2:29
1 Peter 1:22
Romans 6:18   Purity of Heart
Psalm 41:1

The last three blessings go further to calling us into being the type of Christian Jesus prescribes.

[9]Blessed are the peacemakers, for they shall be called sons of God. [10]Blessed are those who are persecuted for righteousness' sake, for theirs is the kingdom of heaven. [11]"Blessed are you when others revile you and persecute you and utter all kinds of evil against you falsely on my account. -Matthew 5: 9-11

Circle the descriptive words in the verses above. What do these people have in common?

_____

_____

Here, Jesus is prioritizing those who prioritize peace. In each of these three verses, we see people who actively pursue peace in counter-cultural ways. In fact, these people go further than just keeping peace, they create peace. As righteousness, mercy, justice, and purity of heart are called out in the previous blessing group, here we are warned against accomplishing those things through violent zealotry. Instead, we are called to turn from retribution or retaliation to reconciliation. Peacemaking is not defined here as being nice or tolerant but as an active entrance into conflict for the purpose of exemplifying the kind of radical reconciliation that God shows us in Christ.

Read the following passages about being a peacemaker and note your reflections on how they aid in creating an attitude of radical reconciliation in your life:

Proverbs 12:20

_____

Romans 14:19

_____

Hebrews 12:14

_____

Inserting ourselves into areas of conflict for the purpose of making peace may yield peace. However, it may also lead to persecution. When we step into the crossfire, we may take some shots.

How does James 5:10 help you to understand the importance of peacemaking even in the context of persecution?

_____

_____

Verbal harassment, injustice, and suffering of all kinds are covered in this blessing group…and assured **twice** of blessing. Please note: this blessing for those who are persecuted is the only one which is repeated.

When we repeat something to a loved one, it's because we know they really need to hear it. How true this is when we are persecuted. Hear our loving Father saying, "I'm here. It's going to be ok; I am right here."

That's a blessing.

Watch Study With Friends Video Series: The Sermon, Episode 2.4

DAY FIVE

THE BLESSING EFFECT

On day two of this week's study, we looked at the three elements of each blessing. Let's return to two of those elements now as we consider the effect of the blessings: the now (earthly) and the future (heavenly).

Dietrich Bonhoeffer describes the ways that we find our blessings complete in the heavenly kingdom of God:

> There shall the poor be seen in the halls of joy. With his own hand God wipes away the tears from the eyes of those who had mourned upon earth. He feeds the hungry at his Banquet. There stand the scarred bodies of the martyrs, now glorified and clothed in the white robes of eternal righteousness instead of the rags of sin and repentance. The echoes of this joy reach the little flock below as it stands beneath the cross and they hear Jesus saying: 'Blessed are ye!' (Bonhoeffer, 1979/1937, p. 114)

Sometimes we can get so caught up in our daily lives that we forget the hope that is in us. This hope indeed exerts itself on our earthly lives, but how much more do we look forward to life in heaven with our Savior? Do we contemplate this often enough for it to make a real impact on how we grasp the hope of the gospel?

Take a few quiet moments to reflect on the hope of heaven and the blessings of God poured out there (don't rush it!).

_____

_____

Our assurance of heaven should affect our lives every day. That takes intentionality because we all so easily fall into the trap of being busy and distracted from the gospel truth, no matter how spiritually mature we might be.

Read the following verses and reflect specifically on how this heavenly truth impacts (or should impact) your day-to-day life:

John 14:2–3

_____

_____

Revelation 7:9–10

_____

_____

Revelation 7:15–17

_____

_____

What are some practical ways you can make the hope of heaven more effective in your daily life?

_____

_____

The other way the blessings take effect is here and now. Jesus assures us in this part of the Sermon that He is blessing us in ways that we and those around us might not expect. John Stott helps us grasp the radical intent of this concept:

> Such a reversal of human values is basic to biblical religion. The ways of the God of the Bible appear topsy-turvy to people. For God exalts the humble and abases the proud, calls the first last and the last first, ascribes greatness to the servant, sends the rich away empty-handed, and declares the meek to be his heirs. The culture of the world and the counterculture of Christ are at loggerheads with each other. In brief, Jesus congratulates those whom the world most pities, and calls the world's rejects 'blessed.' (Stott, 2020, p. 39)

The opposition between how God sees things and how the world sees things is indeed radical. Some might even say unbelievable.

What are some ways that Christians have difficulty accepting the "topsy-turvy" way that God sees us?

_____

_____

What are some ways that the world has difficulty seeing things God's way? Add notes on your understanding of <u>why</u> the world sees things differently.

_____

_____

Use John 17:22-23 to summarize the purpose of Jesus' blessings:

_____

_____

Here is the big news: the blessing effect impacts both Christians *and* those around us. As we will see in our study next week on salt and light, the way that God is working in our lives is evident to those around us even as He is transforming us and blessing us in radical ways. He works *through* us even as He is working *in* us.

Being blessed is kingdom work all around.

Watch Study With Friends Video Series: The Sermon, Episode 2.5

WEEK THREE

KINGDOM INFLUENCE
(MATTHEW 5:13-16)

¹³You are the salt of the earth, but if salt has lost its taste, how shall its saltiness be restored? It is no longer good for anything except to be thrown out and trampled under people's feet. ¹⁴You are the light of the world. A city set on a hill cannot be hidden. ¹⁵Nor do people light a lamp and put it under a basket, but on a stand, and it gives light to all in the house. ¹⁶In the same way, let your light shine before others, so that they may see your good works and give glory to your Father who is in heaven.
–Matthew 5:13-16

This is a segment of the Sermon that is often referred to as the "Salt and Light" passage. It describes the role that we should play in the world and how we should impact those around us.

The metaphors used by Jesus here represent the influential power of God's people in the world. He describes the role of Christians in their culture and community, emphasizing that the actions and attitudes of Christians should be visible to those around them. Disciples of Christ should shine as beacons of hope and guidance, leading others toward a closer relationship with God.

This passage challenges us to live out our faith in a way that has a positive impact on friends, family, coworkers, and anyone we encounter. It reminds us that our actions and attitudes should reflect the love and grace of God. It calls us to be a shining light in a world that so often seems dark. Scot McKnight (2013) says "This text encourages us to reimagine our role in the world as God's agents of redemption."

If this sounds like a tall order, it's a good time to remember the empowerment for this practical Christianity comes from our relationship with Christ and the Spirit that lives in us, not from our own bootstraps.

DAY ONE

THE NEIGHBORHOOD

In attempts to make scripture more readable, Bible translators sometimes provide headings that organize verses into easier-to-digest segments. However, it's important for us to read scripture with an understanding that these headings have been added to the original text.

Take a quick look at the headings you see, starting from the beginning of chapter 5 at least through the end of this week's text.

Note any headings your Bible has added:

_____

Each week we take a small section of scripture and look at it carefully. Let's borrow wisdom from the world of real estate: don't just know the address, know the neighborhood. When you look up a verse on your favorite online Bible search tool and the program asks if you want to read the whole chapter, always say yes. Context matters, and it can illuminate the text in profound ways.

Our passage this week is Matthew 5:13-16, which is the teaching on salt and light. That's what we would call the address. Of course, we already know that this passage is a part of the bigger picture we call the Sermon on the Mount, but it really sits in the broader context of verses 5:10-17 which is what we would call the neighborhood.

Because of the headings added to our Bibles, it may seem unnatural to tie together the end of one section and the beginning of another. But this is the danger of giving too much weight to those headings. The Bible is a very unified narrative, and the broader you look, the more it makes sense. Resist the temptation to artificially segment it.

To really understand verses 13-16, we have to read and understand the preceding verses 10-12 and the following verses 17-20 and make an assumption that they are, in fact, tied together.

Look closely at these surrounding texts to shine a light on this week's core passage.

In verses 10-11, Jesus is talking about persecution. How might that impact the "salt and light" passage?

_____

_____

In verse 19 Jesus warns, "Whoever relaxes one of the least of these commandments and teaches others to do the same will be called least in the kingdom of heaven, but whoever does them and teaches them will be called great in the kingdom of heaven."

What do you think that might mean with respect to the "salt and light" portion of this text?

_____

_____

Does verse 19 remind you of the previous section, the Beatitudes? Why or why not?

_____

_____

_____

Jesus calls us to practical work and promises blessings for keeping His commandments. Let's get down to kingdom business.

Watch Study With Friends Video Series: The Sermon, Episode 3.1

The Sermon
VIDEO SERIES

DAY TWO

PRACTICAL HELP

Salt and light, when used together, are very "churchy" words and concepts. If you have been around church for a while, you have heard them. In fact, sometimes we Christians refer to ourselves as salt and light, and rightly so.

In the Beatitudes, Jesus is very clear about what His disciples should look like. He uses adjectives like meek, merciful, pure…even persecuted.

Having described the *look* of a disciple in the Beatitudes, Jesus warns us now that a disciple who does not *live* this way is worth about as much as tasteless salt or invisible light - nothing. Here, instead of adjectives, He uses metaphors, in this broader context of the neighboring scriptures, to tell us three things:

- Disciples of Christ are called to practical behavior.
- The result could be persecution or persuasion.
- Jesus is serious about good works.

Verses 13-15 talk about practical tools being used in practical ways. Jesus is calling us to do something, not just be something. This underscores the connected nature of our faith and our outward behavior.

What are some examples of practical Christian behavior?

_____

_____

Verse 5:16 shows the desired outcome of our behavior is persuasion, but just before this salt and light passage, in verses 11-12, we also see something about persecution. The result of our salt and light behavior in the world could be persuasion *or* persecution.

We can adopt these practical behaviors and sometimes the people around us will be drawn to our Father in heaven and they will glorify Him. That is the outcome that we want, of course! That people around us would be persuaded to believe in the truth of Christ.

But sometimes the people around us will persecute us. They will belittle us, ridicule us, or worse. They may say things like "Do you *really* believe in all that God stuff?" or "How can you be so naive?"

I once had a friend say she didn't care about whether God exists or not because she didn't feel like she needed to have all the answers. I didn't realize until the car ride home that this was a dig at me, as if my faith was somehow related to my pride.

Are we in America being persecuted? Maybe a *little bit,* because we live in a post-Christian culture that no longer elevates Christianity but largely disdains it. However, there are Christians around the world that are being persecuted in much worse ways. Many of us will never forget the 2015 image of Egyptian Christians in orange jumpsuits on a beach in front of executioners. That is very real persecution. For many, the strength of those believers in the face of real persecution fortified our faith. We thought, if they can do that for their faith, then we can certainly stretch ourselves to talk to a coworker or neighbor about Christ.

Our practical behavior is intended to produce glorification of God, and by His grace, whether we are persuasive or persecuted, our salt and light behavior will serve the same purpose: God's glory.

Do you have any personal examples of radical Christian behavior that deepened your own faith?

The third point we should notice as we look at this passage is that Jesus is serious about good works.

Maybe all of this "good works" talk reminds you of the tricky James passage "faith without works is dead." Perhaps we ask ourselves, "What is the role of work? Do we earn our salvation?" This is why we looked at James and the Sermon side-by-side during week one. Both Jesus and James are talking about the link between faith and work.

We have already noted that the Sermon presupposes that we have a relationship with Christ. It is written to an audience of believers. As such, faith is implied. The works are the result of faith. Faith takes root and produces works.

Paul often talks about the Law and its relationship to Christ. But of course, Jesus says it best in the passage immediately following salt and light.

Read and rephrase Matthew 5:17–20

Said differently, the law turns us to Christ for salvation, and Christ turns us to the law for sanctification. More on this next week.

Jesus freely gives us the grace of salvation, which we need because we all fall short of the perfection required to uphold the law. When we receive this grace, we will naturally become more like Christ in word and deed.

As Bonhoeffer so elegantly said:

> Costly grace is the treasure hidden in the field: for the sake of it a man will gladly go and sell all that he has….it is the kingly rule of Christ…it is the call of Jesus Christ at which the disciple leaves his nets and follows Him…Such grace is *costly* because it calls us to follow, and it is *grace* because it calls us to follow Jesus Christ…Grace is costly because it compels a [person] to submit to the yoke of Christ and follow Him; it is grace because Jesus says: 'My yoke is easy and my burden is light.' (Bonhoeffer, 1979/1937)

Watch Study With Friends Video Series: The Sermon, Episode 3.2

DAY THREE

SALT

There are four ways we should understand salt to get the most out of this passage. Two are commonly understood by most of us, and two might challenge and enlighten us in new ways.

Salt as a Preservative

It is useful to think of salt as something that keeps a bad thing from happening. By applying salt to foods, we can prevent those foods from going bad for a longer period than if they were left unsalted. In this way, we can understand our practical salt application in our own circle of influence. We can look around and decide how to be a preservative.

This may look like a prayerful and careful exhortation about a bad path a friend is heading down. It might look like digging in with God as He works out something in your own life, and being transparent to those around you as you witness to that work. It is often seen as the church collectively working to do good in our communities. In all these ways, we are doing the work Jesus prescribes by preventing evil from taking hold. We are acting like a preservative. Salt.

What are some other ways practical Christian behavior can be a preservative influence in our communities and culture?

_____

Salt as a Flavoring Agent

Another way to think of salt practically is that we flavor our circle of influence, like salt flavors food. In Psalm 34:8 David says "Oh, taste and see that the Lord is good! Blessed is the man who takes refuge in Him!" How can others taste and see that the Lord is good? By getting a taste of our lives. When people see us raising our children, when they see us going to church, when they come to our home and feel welcomed (despite any differences in faith, politics, or lifestyle that may exist between us and them), they get a taste of who Christ is through us. We add a flavor that points people to Christ.

Read Mark 9:50 and note the result that is added in this verse:

_____

_____

What are some other ways practical Christian behavior can be a flavoring influence in our communities and culture?

_____

_____

Salt in Soil

Salt is used in agriculture as an agent to hinder fermentation in manure when that manure is used as a fertilizer, and salt is also used as a fertilizer on its own. This helps us understand the parallel passage in Luke 14:34-35 where Jesus elaborates by saying: [34]"Salt is good, but if salt has lost its taste, how shall its saltiness be restored? [35]It is of no use either for the soil or for the manure pile. It is thrown away. He who has ears to hear, let him hear."

What other examples come to mind where scripture uses agriculture to help us understand the kingdom of God?

_____

_____

If salt is added in some way to the soil to prepare it to grow good things, whether in combination with another fertilizer or as a fertilizer on its own, we can extract from this the idea of being present in the life of a seeker or skeptic for a long time, allowing faith to be well fed, grow, and mature. Sometimes we think of our Christian influence as a sprint, but it's more of a marathon. God calls us to be in the lives of others and to love them well, through ups and downs, as He grows something in their lives (and our own).

Read Colossians 4:6 and note the target of the salt in this verse:

_____

It can be frustrating when a seeker or skeptic takes a long time to see the truth of the gospel, but the idea of practical salt is that we are part of the good soil in which faith can grow.

What are some other ways practical Christian behavior can be a faith-growing influence in our communities and culture?

_____

_____

Salt as Wound Care

For thousands of years sea salt has been recognized as a natural antiseptic and anti-inflammatory and has been used in wound cleansing. Remember the expression, "throwing salt on a wound?" People did this to clean out infected cuts and scrapes. This makes salt a great metaphor for being a comfort to those who are hurting. Rubbing salt in a wound, during biblical times, would have been a good thing.

When we see a wound or hurt in others, how can we apply the salt of our faith in Christ to help them heal?

_____

_____

We might become less salty if we dilute our witness in the culture around us. Think of a person who does great work on Sunday mornings, even serving in the soup kitchen after church. But the Friday before, that person was drunk and involved in a bar fight. Think of a high schooler who regularly goes to church and youth group but has offensive content on their social media accounts. Inconsistency in the life we live can make us less salty.

We have all seen pastors and ministry leaders who become unsalty salt as their personal lives expose some sin that they chose to keep hidden instead of letting Christ deal with it. Unsalty salt is useless for the purpose it was intended to fulfill.

What are some other ways we can become unsalty?

_____

_____

Pray today that God will be so active in your life that you are the saltiest person in your neighborhood.

Watch Study With Friends Video Series: The Sermon, Episode 3.3

DAY FOUR

LIGHT

Light is practical. It's used to see, used for illumination, for dispelling the darkness. Verses 5:14-15 tell us about the practical use of light. Here, Jesus uses two images to reinforce His point. First, the city on the hill. This is a public image.

List some ways that our Christian "light" might be displayed publicly:

_____

_____

Then Jesus talks about light in a home. This is a more private image, reminding us of our closer circle.

List some ways that our Christian "light" might be displayed privately:

_____

_____

But wait, why would you ever put a light under a basket?? Obviously, this is a counterintuitive use of light. We use a light to illuminate, and covering the light takes that purpose away. Like unsalty salt, this is an unbright light. We can see how upside-down those phrases feel.

A literal translation of verse 15 which interprets this "house" as only pertaining to people in our home would be wrong. Those who are in the "house" could be our circle of influence. It could even be another way of saying all who are in the world. But "house" is helpful language when considering our witness to those who do indeed live in our homes. Aren't those people the ones that often see us at our worst?

This is not necessarily a bad thing. Being transparent about our weaknesses gives us an opportunity to show our loved ones how Jesus does His work in real time. The key is going back after unthoughtful words or deeds, letting the person know that we are sorry, and asking God to help us to do better.

It is important to be aware of our behavior in all concentric circles: those closest to us and those most distant. If I see someone once in a department store, I should be the same gospel-carrying, image-bearing person that I am to those who live with me.

A few years ago, my family was driving home from visiting extended family a few hours away. We stopped at a CVS to get a few things, and there was a misunderstanding: I thought someone else was grabbing the bag at checkout and they thought I was grabbing it.

It was about an hour later that we realized we left the bag at CVS. Nothing important, but probably about $30 of items, so I called the store and asked them to refund my card. This was apparently a huge ask.

"We can't do that unless you come back to the store with your card."
"If I was going to come back, I would just get the stuff."
… "Can I talk to the manager?"

I was exhausted and annoyed and apparently, it showed. From the back seat of the car came a quiet voice that said, "Mom, you're not being very nice." It caught me off guard. I *wasn't* being very nice. I wasn't doing my job of salt and light for the store manager, and I wasn't doing it for the people in the car. Being kind matters because we are called to represent Christ and we should take that seriously.

Read John 8:12. Where does our light originate from?

_____

_____

In Matthew 5:16 we note the correlation: by seeing our good deeds people around us will see God and His goodness. In subsequent weeks we will differentiate the motives behind some good deeds but suffice it to say here that the good things we do are designed to cause others to glorify God.

Salt and light have a lot of the same applications. Like when salt is a preservative, light can shine into the dark places to keep something bad from happening. Like when salt is a flavoring agent, light can shine into dark places to help illuminate the person and work of Christ. Like when salt is a fertilizer, light can shine into dark places to allow something good to grow. Like when salt is used for wound care, bringing the light of Christ into places of brokenness is meaningful in a very practical spiritual way.

In all these ways, we become a magnifier of the light of Christ, like when you place a candle in front of a mirror and double its effect. We live in a way that reflects the good news of the kingdom.

Watch Study With Friends Video Series: The Sermon, Episode 3.4

DAY FIVE

BEING AN INFLUENCER

A while back I went to a Journey concert. One of their classic songs is "Lights," and so about ⅓ of the audience turned on their phone flashlights during the performance of that song. I looked around during the song and noticed there was an even spattering of lights around the arena. Even though not all concertgoers were holding up a phone, enough of them were to distribute the light well. There were no large collections of light, and neither were there any large sections where no light existed. This simple action created a sense of community among the audience members, most of whom were strangers to each other.

I looked up to see if they had raised the house lights so that the band could see the audience because it was noticeably more well-lit in the arena. It was then that I realized that all these little lights, each smaller than a pencil eraser, were doing an incredible job as a collective: lighting an arena that seats about 20,000 people. This is a great example of salt and light.

The light was perceptible. Not everyone in the arena was holding up a phone, and not every person in the world is a Christian. Each person holding up a light had done their little part to light their own small section, but the collective effect was a measurable difference-maker. Yes, our passage calls us to be the salt and light of the world, but none of us is responsible for the entire world, only the places where God calls us personally to be.

We start where we are. We look for places where we can increase Christ's influence. We pay attention to the things that we are doing in public and in private and ask for God's help in aligning those behaviors to the pattern of Christ. In this way, we individually light a small spot and collectively light the world. This is an exhortation to have public faith and to do it for God's glory.

Jesus talks about this beyond the Sermon on the Mount and when He does, He often uses the metaphor of a tree.

Read Matthew 7:17–20 and Matthew 12:33. Compare the tree analogies to the salt/light analogies. Note the similarities and the differences.

_____

_____

_____

_____

Paul David Tripp (2005) tells a great story to help us understand this better. I will paraphrase it for you.

There was a man who had an apple tree in his front yard. Because it was in his front yard, all his neighbors would go by it on a regular basis, often commenting on the beautiful, plentiful apples that always seemed to be evident on the tree. The man was very happy to have his tree appreciated this way.

One day he noticed that some of the apples were losing their color. A few weeks later, he noticed several apples were falling off the tree before getting fully ripe. About a month after that, he could see the apples were neither growing nor were they ripening, and overall, there were just fewer apples on the tree. His neighbors noticed too.

This man just knew that his tree was the highest example of an apple tree that his neighbors would ever see. He knew that if they could not see his tree in full apple amazingness, they would begin to wonder what value apples even had and whether apples were important at all. He simply could not have that.

So, each day, late in the afternoon, he would go to the grocery store and purchase all the big, red apples that he could carry home. Then, late at night, when all his neighbors were asleep, he would go out with his ladder and basket of apples and staple the good apples onto the tree.

Of course, stapled apples don't stick, so by late afternoon the next day, all the apples had fallen off, and he had to do it all over again. In this way, he solved the problem of his apple tree producing good fruit. Or did he?

Would it have been better for him to look at the health of the tree, the trunk, the roots, and the soil where the tree was planted to find the problem that was causing the apples to shrivel up? Of course it would have. A root problem cannot be fixed with a surface solution. This is what Jesus means by a tree being known by its fruit. God wants our spiritual health, our biblical roots, and the grace-filled soil where we are planted to produce real and lasting fruit.

Where are you stapling apples in your life?

_____

_____

How do the larger culture and even the church culture create an environment where we feel we need to staple apples onto our tree?

_____

_____

A wrong application of the salt and light passage can sometimes be to blame for people feeling compelled to look fruitful, even when they know something deeper is causing a problem with their fruit.

Write out John 15:5 as a reminder of where fruit starts in our lives:

_____

_____

_____

The gospel is not intended to serve as a behavior modification process on its own. Our daily awareness of the grace of God naturally produces different behaviors in us, resulting in salt and light for the world. But if we try to fix the behavior without letting grace do its work first it's the same as stapling apples to a tree instead of fixing the roots: it doesn't work. And honestly, it's exhausting. Our practical good works must be gospel-driven and not self-driven.

Let's close this week with the encouragement of John 1:5: *The light shines in the darkness, and the darkness has not overcome it.*

Watch Study With Friends Video Series: The Sermon, Episode 3.5

WEEK FOUR
CHRIST AND THE LAW
(MATTHEW 5:17-20)

¹⁷ Do not think that I have come to abolish the Law or the Prophets; I have not come to abolish them but to fulfill them. ¹⁸ For truly, I say to you, until heaven and earth pass away, not an iota, not a dot, will pass from the Law until all is accomplished. ¹⁹ Therefore whoever relaxes one of the least of these commandments and teaches others to do the same will be called least in the kingdom of heaven, but whoever does them and teaches them will be called great in the kingdom of heaven. ²⁰ For I tell you, unless your righteousness exceeds that of the scribes and Pharisees, you will never enter the kingdom of heaven.
–Matthew 5:17-20

This week's passage emphasizes the sovereignty of God and the centrality of Christ in salvation.

Note the progression of the Sermon thus far and how it has narrowed in focus. In the Beatitudes, Jesus says "Blessed are..." in broad terms. In the Salt and Light passage, He says "You are..." Now He appears to lean in and say "I tell you..." and again "for I tell you..." so that we might notice His directness and receive the significant teaching: <u>In this passage, Jesus teaches us how to understand the entire Bible.</u>

But what does this relationship between Christ and the Law mean for Christians today? Jesus' fulfillment of the Law does not mean that Christians are free to disregard the Law's moral commands. On the contrary, the moral laws of the Old Testament are still applicable today. Christ fulfilled the law and, having been united with Christ by the Spirit, we now walk in that fulfillment. This means ritual law is no longer necessary but moral law is. As Christians, we are called to follow God's commands and to live righteous lives. The Sermon makes that plain.

This is where Christ comes in. Through faith in Jesus, we are justified before God, and we are declared righteous in God's sight. This is the central message of the Gospel.

The Law teaches us that we need a Savior, and that Savior is Jesus Christ.

DAY ONE

THE LAW

The Law was given through Moses, and it included moral and ceremonial laws. The moral laws dealt with ethical behavior, such as the Ten Commandments. The ceremonial laws were given to the Israelites to guide them in their worship of God. These laws included regulations about sacrifices, festivals, and other religious practices. Jesus intentionally includes both Moses and the prophets, so that it is clear to us that the entire Torah/Law is being addressed in these verses of the Sermon.

Read the following passages and note with an M or C whether the instructions were moral or ceremonial:

Genesis 32:32	Leviticus 12:3
Exodus 12:15	Leviticus 25:9
Exodus 20:3	Numbers 9:12
Exodus 20:12	Deuteronomy 16:16
Exodus 20:13	Deuteronomy 24:5
Exodus 22:9	Deuteronomy 31:12

Are you surprised to see the Law be so specific in what it addresses? Why or why not?

_____

_____

Read Romans 3:19-20 and note the duality of the Law described there. What does the Law make us aware of?

_____

What is the Law unable to do?

_____

The Old Testament Law was comprehensive, but still unable to save people from their sins. No one could perfectly obey the Law, and therefore, all were guilty before God. What the Law was able to do was show us our sins and teach us about ourselves in that way. In this sense, the Law was a "schoolmaster" that pointed people to their need for a savior.

Read Galatians 3:23-26. How does this passage help you to understand the relationship between Christ and the Law?

———————————————————————————————————

———————————————————————————————————

Jesus, as the fulfillment of the Law, came to bring salvation to God's people. He did not come to abolish the Law, but to fulfill it. This means that He perfectly obeyed the Law in every way, both morally and ceremonially. He fulfilled the prophecies, types, and shadows of the Law found in the Old Testament.

Romans 10:5-13 expands on the reach of Christ's work. What do you see in this passage that extends the work of Christ beyond what the Old Testament Law provided?

———————————————————————————————————

———————————————————————————————————

Through His perfect obedience, Jesus accomplished what no one else could: He became the perfect sacrifice for sin. By His death on the cross, He satisfied the penalty for sin that the Law demanded. In this way, Jesus' fulfillment of the Law was the ultimate act of obedience to God. But beyond the Old Testament Law, which was given to the Israelites, Christ came to save all.

Watch Study With Friends Video Series: The Sermon, Episode 4.1

DAY TWO

NOT TO ABOLISH

One of the most important statements in the Sermon is found in 5:17, where Jesus says, "Do not think that I have come to abolish the Law or the Prophets; I have not come to abolish them but to fulfill them." Notice how He creates emphasis by saying *twice* that He did not come to abolish the Law or Prophets.

What is your initial impression about why Jesus would say this twice?

There are two reasons Jesus may have felt it was important to emphasize this point. One is cultural and specific to that time (but still very useful for us to understand in the context of the whole Bible), and the other is a broader truth about human nature.

First, Jesus may have felt it was important to underscore His support for the Law and the Prophets because of the way that the Pharisees (the "specialists" in the Law) held so tightly to their understanding of the Law. In many cases, Jesus' message and actions seemed to be opposed to the Law and the Pharisees.

Read each passage and note how the circumstances might have placed Jesus in conflict with the Pharisees and/or their understanding of the Law:

Matthew 4:23–25

Mark 2:23–28

Mark 3:1-6

Each of these passages shows different ways that Jesus might have been perceived as an opposing force to the rule and authority of the Pharisees and the Law. In each case, and here in the Sermon, Jesus is attempting to help them see that He is not opposed to them, but that they have their understanding wrong. He wanted them to see!

In the last passage, Mark 3:5 says that Jesus "looked around at them with anger, grieved at their hardness of heart." This is an insightful moment, showing that Jesus felt frustration over the stubbornness of the Pharisees. The root of that frustration is easy to understand: Jesus came to do a saving work for His people. At the time, the leaders of His people were the Pharisees, yet even they could not see who Jesus was and what He was trying to teach them.

Jesus expresses this frustration differently in Matthew 23:37. How does this passage illuminate Christ's heart for all, including the Pharisees?

Considering these passages, we can see why Jesus would have felt it important to emphasize His partnership, rather than enmity, with the Law.

The second reason that Jesus may have felt it important to emphasize that He did not come to abolish the Law is the natural human propensity to embrace the new and cast aside the old. Before Jesus says He came to fulfill the Law, He says twice that He did *not* come to abolish it. The claim that Jesus was fulfilling the Law and Prophets could easily have been received as an implication that the Torah no longer mattered. But Jesus says exactly the opposite.

As we noted on day one this week, Jesus intentionally includes both the Law and Prophets in His statement, which means He is speaking of the entire Old Testament. On day four this week we will dive into the implications of that, but for now, let's focus on what He is really saying: take the Law seriously. In fact, this segment of the Sermon sets up verses 21-48 where Jesus tightens the parameters of the Law, ending with a command for us to be perfect!

Taken in the context of the whole Sermon, we can't possibly think that Jesus came to redefine or relax the Law and the Prophets in any way. Instead, He came to enlighten us about the purpose of the Law, about our own condition, and about God's plan for how to reconcile the two.

If there was any doubt about how much Jesus embraced the Law and Prophets, we might use Matthew 17:1-3 to dispel that doubt.

What do Moses and Elijah represent in this passage?

_____

_____

What do you think this scripture was meant to portray, especially the last three words of verse three (ESV)?

_____

_____

No, Jesus did not come to abolish the Law and Prophets. He loves them both, and God gave them for our good and His glory.

Watch Study With Friends Video Series: The Sermon, Episode 4.2

DAY THREE

To Fulfill

Keeping with the theme that Matthew 5:17 is extremely impactful and important to understand, we move today from the narrative that Jesus did not come to abolish the Law and Prophets to His statement that He came to fulfill them. It's a big statement.

How do we think of fulfillment in our current culture? Can you think of some secular things that are "fulfilled?"

_____

Do these fulfillments help us to understand what Jesus was saying? Why or why not?

_____

Jesus was not just fulfilling prophecy (though He was certainly doing that), He was reorienting the way we look at the Old Testament in its entirety. This is what disturbed some of His contemporaries, and it's what disturbs some people even today. Despite the accusations we studied on day two, verse 5:17 of the Sermon boldly states the truth: Jesus is the central story of all scripture.

Those of us who are "churched" may miss the magnitude of this statement, but we should pause to meditate on it. By fulfilling all the Old Testament, Jesus teaches us how to read both the Old and New Testament, recognizing that all scripture points to Jesus. Declaring that He has come to fulfill the Law and the Prophets is the ultimate embodiment of the phrase "hindsight is 20/20."

Jesus reiterates this truth to some of His disciples on the road to Emmaus. Read Luke 24:13-27.

How does this section of scripture help you understand Jesus' fulfillment of the Law and Prophets?

_____

_____

Are there any additional elements in the Luke passage that add to Matthew 5:17?

_____

_____

Read Jeremiah 31:31–34. Reflect on the personal ways that this passage speaks to you about Jesus as the fulfillment of the Old Testament:

_____

_____

Jesus was not sent to fulfill the Law and the Prophets just so that God could say, "told you so!" He was sent because God loves us so deeply that He wanted to reveal Himself to us, have intimacy with us, and be reconciled with us.

What great love.

Watch Study With Friends Video Series: The Sermon, Episode 4.3

DAY FOUR

EVERYTHING

With barely a breath between verses 5:17 and 18, Jesus moves from proclaiming Himself the fulfillment to explaining the way that we understand and apply that fulfillment to the whole of scripture. In doing so, He doubles down on the Old Testament. In verse 18, Jesus is saying everything in the Old Testament is true *in the context of Jesus being that fulfillment.* If this is the case (and it is), it changes how we read the entire bible.

Generally, we find Old Testament truth in three categories: it teaches *doctrine*, provides *prophecy*, and defines *ethics*.

Doctrine is instruction about God, humanity, salvation, etc. Read the following Old Testament passages and note your understanding of the doctrine explained or implied:

Proverbs 4:2

_____

Jeremiah 10:8

_____

Deuteronomy 32:2

_____

Partnering the above Old Testament verses with Hebrews 1:1-2, write your reflections on how the person and work of Jesus Christ ratify Old Testament doctrine:

_____

_____

The Old Testament also contains *prophecies* that are fulfilled in Christ. Here are a few examples:

Prophecy: Isaiah 35:5–6…Fulfillment: Matthew 11:2–6
Prophecy: Leviticus 17:11…Fulfillment: Matthew 26:28
Prophecy: 1 Samuel 2:35…Fulfillment: Hebrews 2:17

Partnering the above Old Testament verses with the following passages, write your reflections on how the person and work of Jesus Christ ratify Old Testament prophecy:

Mark 1:15

_____

_____

Colossians 2:17

_____

_____

The Old Testament also contains a code of *ethics*. This is the moral law of God and a roadmap to how we might accomplish righteousness and redemption.

We are all surely familiar with the example of the Ten Commandments, but read these other verses and note your understanding of the ethical command:

Leviticus 19:13

_____

_____

Proverbs 11:1

_____

_____

Psalm 25:21

_____

_____

Partnering the above Old Testament verses with the following passages, write your reflections on how the person and work of Jesus Christ ratify Old Testament ethics:

Galatians 4:4-5

_____

_____

Matthew 3:13-15

_____

_____

We often think of the ways that Jesus fulfilled Old Testament prophecy. But also, in the area of doctrine and ethics, the revelation of Jesus Christ provides a true completion of the Old Testament. By living among us, He exponentially deepened our doctrinal understanding of who God is. Through His work on the cross, He brings us into a restored relationship with God, even as He simultaneously equips us to be better keepers of the Law.

Watch Study With Friends Video Series: The Sermon, Episode 4.4

DAY FIVE

WITH OBEDIENCE

Speaking of our equipping to be better keepers of the Law, in verses 19-20 we get an unapologetic picture of the expectation there, and the standard is high. Jesus again admonishes His disciples not to relax our hold on the Law, explaining that to do so would be an offense to God. He warns that our obedience to the Law must exceed the legal experts. Throughout the Sermon, Jesus uses strong language and firm statements to remind us of what discipleship should look like.

How can it be that discipleship means adherence to Christ alone, yet also means being bound to the Old Testament law? Bonhoeffer asks, "Which is our final authority, Christ or the law? To which are we bound? Christ had said that no law was to be allowed to come between Him and His disciples. Now he tells us that to abandon the Law would be to separate ourselves from Him. What exactly does he mean?" (Bonhoeffer, 1979/1937, p. 121).

What are your initial reflections on how being a disciple of Christ also means being bound to the Law?

_____

_____

The early church grappled with how to synthesize the Law and the gospel. A great example of this is found in Acts 10:1-11:18.

Who are the main characters in this passage?

_____

What was the core of the difference in their perspectives at the beginning of this narrative?

_____

How were their differences resolved?

_____

Both men had a supernatural experience that brought them together. No one other than the Lord Himself would have been as persuasive, especially for willful Peter.

What is your takeaway from this passage about the gospel and the law?

_____

_____

Paul exemplifies a fuller understanding of the balance between law and gospel and shares that with his friends in Corinth.

Read 1 Corinthians 9:19-23. Do you think that this passage shows Paul as a watered-down preacher? Why or why not?

_____

_____

Paul understands that the heart of the Law is, in fact, the gospel of Christ. He understands that the law exerts itself on us through doctrine, prophecy, and ethics, but should not put us in chains to outward obedience. This is what Jesus is explaining in verse 20 when He tells us that our obedience must exceed that of the Pharisees and scribes. The Pharisees had calculated the law into 248 commandments and 365 prohibitions. Then they went about figuring out how to keep those laws. But the gospel of Christ is a law written on our *hearts*.

Reflect on how these passages separate the outward appearance from the inward motivations:

1 Samuel 16:7

_____

_____

Luke 16:15

_____

_____

The gospel/law balance that is fulfilled in Christ is the law that was promised in Jeremiah 31:33 and Ezekiel 36:27.

Read those passages and summarize your understanding of what was promised:

_____

_____

How does a practical understanding of the balance between the gospel and the Law inform our understanding of the previous passages of the Sermon (like the Beatitudes and the Salt and Light passage)?

_____

_____

When the Spirit lives in us, through Christ, we don't abandon the Law. Rather, the Spirit writes God's Law on our hearts and minds, causing us to be truly new creations, with new motivations and new actions. Our adoption of the Law is not a behavioral modification program working from the outside in. It's the evidence of a truly transformed heart.

This righteousness is the evidence of new birth in Christ, and it exceeds the righteousness of the scribes and Pharisees because it is Christ's perfect righteousness which no human could ever accomplish. This is what James is describing when he says in 2:10: *"whoever keeps the whole law but fails in one point has become accountable for all of it."* Those who are concerned with accomplishing righteousness by external behavior will only be justified if they keep all 613 laws perfectly, every day, for their whole lives.

In John 3:3 a Pharisee named Nicodemus was struggling to understand what Jesus was teaching. Jesus answered him, "Truly, truly, I say to you, unless one is born again he cannot see the kingdom of God."

The kingdom of God is governed by the laws of God. It requires full acceptance of the gospel of Christ for citizenship.

Watch Study With Friends Video Series: The Sermon, Episode 4.5

WEEK FIVE

Kingdom Behavior
(Matthew 5:21-48)

[21] *You have heard that it was said to those of old, 'You shall not murder; and whoever murders will be liable to judgment.'* [22] *But I say to you that everyone who is angry with his brother will be liable to judgment; whoever insults his brother will be liable to the council; and whoever says, 'You fool!' will be liable to the hell of fire.* [23] *So if you are offering your gift at the altar and there remember that your brother has something against you,* [24] *leave your gift there before the altar and go. First be reconciled to your brother, and then come and offer your gift.* [25] *Come to terms quickly with your accuser while you are going with him to court, lest your accuser hand you over to the judge, and the judge to the guard, and you be put in prison.* [26] *Truly, I say to you, you will never get out until you have paid the last penny.* [27] *You have heard that it was said, 'You shall not commit adultery.'* [28] *But I say to you that everyone who looks at a woman with lustful intent has already committed adultery with her in his heart.* [29] *If your right eye causes you to sin, tear it out and throw it away. For it is better that you lose one of your members than that your whole body be thrown into hell.* [30] *And if your right hand causes you to sin, cut it off and throw it away. For it is better that you lose one of your members than that your whole body go into hell.* [31] *It was also said, 'Whoever divorces his wife, let him give her a certificate of divorce.'* [32] *But I say to you that everyone who divorces his wife, except on the ground of sexual immorality, makes her commit adultery, and whoever marries a divorced woman commits adultery.* [33] *Again you have heard that it was said to those of old, 'You shall*

not swear falsely, but shall perform to the Lord what you have sworn.' [34] But I say to you, Do not take an oath at all, either by heaven, for it is the throne of God, [35] or by the earth, for it is his footstool, or by Jerusalem, for it is the city of the great King. [36] And do not take an oath by your head, for you cannot make one hair white or black. [37] Let what you say be simply 'Yes' or 'No'; anything more than this comes from evil. [38] You have heard that it was said, 'An eye for an eye and a tooth for a tooth.' [39] But I say to you, Do not resist the one who is evil. But if anyone slaps you on the right cheek, turn to him the other also. [40] And if anyone would sue you and take your tunic, let him have your cloak as well. [41] And if anyone forces you to go one mile, go with him two miles. [42] Give to the one who begs from you, and do not refuse the one who would borrow from you. [43] You have heard that it was said, 'You shall love your neighbor and hate your enemy.' [44] But I say to you, Love your enemies and pray for those who persecute you, [45] so that you may be sons of your Father who is in heaven. For He makes His sun rise on the evil and on the good, and sends rain on the just and on the unjust. [46] For if you love those who love you, what reward do you have? Do not even the tax collectors do the same? [47] And if you greet only your brothers, what more are you doing than others? Do not even the Gentiles do the same? [48] You therefore must be perfect, as your heavenly Father is perfect.
–Matthew 5:21–48

After strenuously upholding the Old Testament Law in verses 17-20, Jesus now tightens the grip on our application of it. Each section of this passage is a powerful message about the importance of righteousness and purity in the life of a believer. Here, Jesus' teachings challenge traditional interpretations of the Law and emphasize the need for a deeper understanding of God's heart and intentions. This portion of the Sermon serves as a reminder that following the letter of the Law is not enough, but that true obedience requires a commitment to the spirit of the Law as well.

DAY ONE

THE CONTRASTS

Jesus repeats a cadence in this segment of the Sermon which draws a stark contrast between the previous understanding of the Law and His new revelation of it. His use of the phrase "You have heard…but I say…" gives us a good way to put the teaching into two columns: here is what you think, and here is what I am teaching you.

Review Matthew 5:21–48. Who or what is Jesus contrasting here?

_____

_____

During week four we spent a significant amount of our time and attention on the fact that Jesus was not debunking the Law or setting Himself up against Moses. As we read this week's passage, we must remember that He is not introducing something new and casting off something old. Instead, He is endorsing the law, affirming its authority, and providing its true interpretation.

Both the Sadducees and the Pharisees had adopted misrepresentations of the Law. Jesus provides much-needed clarification - and He does not mince words doing it. For example, later in the book of Matthew, some Sadducees ask Jesus about His teaching. He answers by saying, "You are wrong, because you know neither the Scriptures nor the power of God." (Matthew 22:29).

What are some ways that the culture and even the church might get the Scriptures and the power of God wrong?

_____

_____

What implications can this have on our ability to adopt the precepts of the Sermon in our everyday life?

_____

_____

Jesus held the Old Testament in high regard and so should we. It provides teaching that is practical for use in life's toughest trials. Just before the Sermon appears in the book of Matthew, another narrative shows us the value Christ places on the usefulness and power of the Old Testament.

Read Matthew 4:1–11. What is Jesus' response to each of the devil's temptations?

_____

_____

Reflect on ways Matthew 4:1–11, in the context of the Sermon, empowers us to adopt and apply Jesus' teachings:

_____

_____

Jesus is our prophet, priest, and king. His example of the way the Law applies to us is important to follow. His commands in the verses that follow might seem impossible to accomplish. We can do these things through Christ alone, we do them by His strength not ours, and we do them for His glory.

Watch Study With Friends Video Series: The Sermon, Episode 5.1

DAY TWO

VALUE GOD'S IMAGE-BEARERS

Matthew 5:21-26 is the beginning of how Jesus will unfold the meaning behind verse 20 where He commands us to exceed the obedience of the scribes and Pharisees. Here, He starts the work of defining (or expanding the definition of) Old Testament Law. He begins with anger, but to say this segment is solely about anger is reductive. This passage is about respecting, protecting, preserving, and celebrating human life. It teaches us what that level of value really looks like.

God surely speaks to anger elsewhere in the Bible. Read the following passages and summarize the message of each.

Ecclesiastes 7:9

_____

Psalm 37:8

_____

Ephesians 4:26-27, 31

_____

James 1:19-20

_____

In this part of the Sermon, the ethical command against anger is connected to the prohibition of murder in the sixth commandment. Jesus is helping us understand the kind of sinful anger that leads not just to murder, but also to insult and abuse (v. 22).

Let's start with the elephant in the room on this one: war and the death penalty. These are typically debated by treatments of the sixth commandment, however, to avoid it here would be remiss. All throughout the Bible, God teaches us to have respect for life. We are shown that each human bears the image of God and is His workmanship (Genesis 1:26-27; Psalms 139:14, etc.) and that He highly values us - so we should value each other. Therefore, the demand for justice is based on the high value of human life.

Read Genesis 9:6 and write your reflections on how this passage relates to anger and justice.

_____

_____

Read James 3:9 and reflect on how this passage relates to anger and justice.

_____

_____

Read Romans 13:1 and note the role of government in justice.

_____

_____

War and the death penalty are complex issues. Biblical scholars have written volumes of books dedicated to understanding how these issues are included or excluded from biblical ethics and morality. We should prayerfully pursue that thread outside of this study space, but here we will suffice it to say that this section of the Sermon does not overturn justice and the punishment of evildoers.

It also does not prohibit righteous anger. God Himself is sometimes angry.

Read Jeremiah 19:2-9 and describe why God is angry:

_____

_____

How, then, do we discern for ourselves which anger is prohibited and which is accepted? In week one we talked about how scripture teaches scripture. Let's apply that again here.

Read Galatians 5:19-24. What are your preliminary thoughts on how this might apply to different types of anger?

_____

_____

In Matthew 5:21-26, Jesus is teaching us to avoid *sinful* anger. Said differently, this is anger that is rooted in sins like pride, envy, strife, rivalry, dissension, division, drunkenness, etc. (Galatians 5:19-21). On the other hand, righteous anger is rooted in righteousness. We can (and should) be angry anytime we see biblical injustice, disrespect for human life, or behaviors that don't embody love, joy, peace, patience, kindness, goodness, faithfulness, gentleness, and self-control (Galatians 5:22-23).

Juxtaposing these two segments of scripture does not make the command to practical discipleship about anger easier to accomplish, but it gives us a roadmap to identify anger that is approved and anger that is prohibited. It also reminds us that we do so by the strength of the Spirit (Galatians 5:18).

The second segment of the Sermon's teaching on anger is a call to radical reconciliation. This further emphasizes the command to respect, protect, and preserve both human life *and* the quality of that life. The goal Jesus commands here is to live with such radical and intentional reconciliation that it becomes a lifestyle.

Prayerfully consider the following questions, then put down this study to take the necessary steps to restore harmony, because Jesus instructs us to interrupt our life and make it a priority to be reconciled (Matthew 5:23-26):

Is there anyone for whom you harbor bitterness or resentment?

_____

Is there anyone who might hold a grudge against you right now?

_____

Is there anyone with whom you are not fully reconciled?

Pray also about the offenses you have caused without your own awareness. Ask God to strengthen the relationships in your life so that each party always feels safe to bring any issue to the table, pursuing radical reconciliation and peace as the rule and not the exception.

Watch Study With Friends Video Series: The Sermon, Episode 5.2

DAY THREE

VALUE INTIMACY

A reasonable summary of Matthew 5:27-32 is that Jesus is commanding us to value the gift of intimacy between a husband and a wife. In that light, verses 27-30 warn against "lustful intent" and verses 31-32 warn against taking divorce lightly. The entire passage recalls the seventh and tenth commandments, but again, Jesus expands on what those commands really mean.

Once again, the rabbis of the time were attempting to limit the scope of the commandments. Prohibiting only the act of adultery itself (seventh commandment) and relaxing the meaning of coveting a neighbor's wife (tenth commandment) allowed a conveniently narrow view of sexual sin and a conveniently broad definition of sexual purity (Stott, 2020, p. 67). Jesus broadens our understanding of sexual immorality to show us that anything unlawful in deed is also unlawful in thought or desire. He also points out where those desires begin.

Read Job 31:1-10. Note the connection Job made between his eyes and his heart:

_____

_____

Contrast the above Job passage with 2 Peter 2:14. Note the behavior of false prophets and deceivers:

_____

_____

All three of these passages point out that sin starts with the gaze of our eyes upon something that we desire with our hearts. Job proclaims that he made a covenant with his eyes to pursue righteousness. This is the discipline Jesus is calling us to adopt. By the way, this applies to both men and women, so be sure not to dismiss it as applying to men only.

Read 1 Corinthians 6:13-20, focusing on 19-20. What is the connection between this passage and the teaching on lust in the Sermon?

_____

_____

This portion of the Sermon is a reminder to be aware of our sexual temptations and avoid them, to notice the connection between our eyes and our hearts, and to take preemptive action to avoid sin. As John Stott (2020, p. 71) puts it, "We have to decide, quite simply, whether to live for this world or the next, whether to follow the crowd or Jesus Christ."

This passage is not just prohibiting impurity, it is elevating purity and the gift of intimacy that God has given us. The entire book of Song of Solomon is a testimony to the beauty of intimacy.

Read Song of Solomon 7:1-10. What are your reflections on the sacredness of this intimacy?

_____

_____

Sadly, the Song of Solomon is often neglected when teaching biblical standards for marriage and intimacy. We often focus too much on the "do not" and not enough on the "do," but God has provided us with a clear picture of purity and intimacy. By denouncing the impure, Jesus has elevated the proper view of intimacy.

Matthew 5:31-32 goes on to teach about divorce. There are resources in Appendix B which have better treatments of this passage than we have space for here. If you or a loved one are facing the issue of divorce, please consider these resources. For now, we will attempt to understand the basic premise of what Jesus is teaching in this section of the Sermon.

Read Deuteronomy 24:1-4 (which is the text Jesus is referring to in Matthew 5:31). Note the main points:

_____

_____

Now read Matthew 19:3-9 and note what Jesus is doing with the above Deuteronomy passage:

_____

_____

As we ponder this section of the Sermon, we must grasp three biblical precepts:

First, marriage is a covenant and God takes covenants very seriously, so a divorce destroys something that God highly values.

Read and paraphrase Mark 10:9:

_____

_____

Second, marriage is based on selfless love, which is the kind of discipleship Jesus is teaching in the Sermon, so a divorce destroys that element of discipleship.

Read and paraphrase Philippians 2:3-4 in the context of marriage:

_____

_____

Third, all throughout the bible, God uses marriage as a reflection of His love for His people, so a divorce destroys the reflection of God who is completely faithful.

Read Ephesians 5:25-29 and note your reflections here:

_____

_____

What are some ways we can diminish the value of intimacy in our own lives or the lives of others?

_____

_____

Divorce and remarriage are much more complicated than we can get into in a broader study of the Sermon, and these issues affect the real lives of men, women, and children every day. The best we can hope for here is an understanding that God desires for us to behave selflessly inside the marriage covenant so that we can honor Him and honor each other.

When a marriage no longer displays this kind of selflessness due to adultery, abuse, or desertion, divorce may be on the table. Seeking pastoral care in a situation where you or a loved one are facing this issue is the wisest course.

Watch Study With Friends Video Series: The Sermon, Episode 5.3

DAY FOUR

LIVE TRUTHFULLY

In verses 5:33-37 of the Sermon, Jesus teaches about oaths and the value of truth. What is an oath?

Bonhoeffer (1979/1937, p. 136) says, "It is an appeal made to God in public, calling upon Him to witness a statement made in connection with an event or fact, past, present, or future." In this teaching, Jesus reminds us that every word we speak is witnessed by God, not just those we utter more strenuously through an oath of some kind. Therefore, every word we say should be honest and upright before the Lord.

Read Deuteronomy 23:21-23 and summarize the command:

_____

_____

Israel began to organize under Moses as an established community with laws, and there were basic human behaviors that had to be addressed. The Ten Commandments are the beginning of this organization, and the more granular prohibitions and commands in the rest of the Torah are also put in place to accomplish an ordered community. Read the following passages in the context of the ninth commandment. All these passages would have been very well known by the nation of Israel during Moses' time. Summarize the lies that were told:

Genesis 12:10-20

_____

Genesis 27:1-40

_____

Genesis 29:1-30

Genesis 37:12-36

Do you notice any common threads in these narratives, aside from dishonesty?

During the time that Jesus taught the Sermon, the Pharisees had contorted the Law and created confusion over how to obey it. Jesus is clearing up that confusion with better teaching.

Matthew 23:16-22 gives more insight. What do you notice about this passage?

The teaching from Matthew 23 shows that oaths in that culture had become too complicated to be meaningful. They had become a scale by which the commitment of the speaker could be measured. But what Jesus is pointing out here is the fundamental problem with that scale: it is based on an assumed lack of honesty. If we must add layers of oaths to our statements it means when we don't, we can't be trusted.

Even today, interpretations of law can create additions, exclusions, addendums, and the like. We encounter all sorts of different experiences that cause us to look at the law differently and we try to accommodate every eventuality by adding layer upon layer to the original law. Jesus mercifully decodes the complications and makes it plain: absolute honesty is the standard for His disciples.

The early church took this seriously. On the surface, the James passage which is parallel to this part of the Sermon does not seem to add much in the way of expanding this teaching or even paraphrasing it. However, the first three words of James 5:12 offer important insight.

Write those first three words from James 5:12 (ESV) and note the distinction:

James says that truth should be prioritized above all.

Throughout this study we have referenced work by Dietrich Bonhoeffer, who lived through World War 2 under the Nazi regime. He grappled with truth on a completely different level than most of us do each day. Faced with the atrocities of this war, is answering the Nazi questions truthfully what Jesus' disciples are called to do? If asked, "Are you hiding any Jews?" should the answer be yes because that is the truth?

What are your thoughts on prioritizing truth in difficult circumstances?

In his book *Ethics,* Bonhoeffer allowed for "necessary deception of the enemy in war," (Bonhoeffer, 1955/1949) understanding the deeper truths that God calls us to honor. Bonhoeffer asks us to:

- Recognize who is calling us to speak, and what authorizes us to speak.
- Recognize the place in which we stand.
- Put the subject we are speaking about into this context.

In this way, we may honor a larger Biblical truth like the preservation of life by not telling the truth about hiding or protecting a certain people group from government-sanctioned genocide.

Accepting that, we find ourselves at the top of a slippery slope and should not leave this day's study with an understanding that we get to choose when we lie and when we tell the truth. This is exactly what Jesus is prohibiting. Dietrich Bonhoeffer produced an extensive number of sermons, books, and essays on theological and ethical dilemmas. Those works do a much better job than we can in the small space allotted here. *Ethics* is recommended for anyone who wants to dive deeper into the complications of living truthfully in difficult times.

Watch Study With Friends Video Series: The Sermon, Episode 5.4

DAY FIVE

PRIORITIZE LOVE

Matthew 5:38-42 seems to speak of justice and 43-48 of love, but in fact, they both teach that love is the way to deal with evil and opposition.

McKnight says the word justice is "used for conditions and behaviors that conform to the standards or the laws at work in a particular society" (McKnight, 2013, p. 121). A staple of justice is punishment or consequences that are equal to the crime.

Write your own definition of the word "justice."

_____

Read Exodus 21:23-25 and Leviticus 24:19-20. Note the relationship between the crime and the punishment:

_____

_____

In these passages, retribution is limited but equal to the original injury. This rule helps to curb violence and prevent vengeance from being disproportionate.

Read Genesis 4:23-24 and describe the offense and the retribution:

_____

_____

Deuteronomy 19:21 instructs the nation of Israel to "show no pity" when dispensing this justice that is equal to the crime. This passage describes capital punishment (life for life) and corporal punishment (eye for eye, tooth for tooth, etc.).

How does this law square up against the teaching Jesus is providing in Matthew 5:38-42? Is Jesus disposing of justice in the Sermon? No. God is full of justice. Rather, Jesus is elevating love and peace as the best way to diffuse evil.

Bonhoeffer explains, "The followers of Jesus for His sake renounce every personal right. He calls them blessed because they are meek. If after giving up everything else for His sake they still wanted to cling to their own rights, they would then have ceased to follow Him. This passage, therefore, is simply an elaboration of the beatitudes" (Bonhoeffer, 1979/1937, p. 140).

Jesus' words "do not resist an evil person" hold an implication of <u>both non-resistance and active love</u>. He is advocating here for adherence to preexisting Bible themes.

Read Leviticus 19:18, Proverbs 20:22, and 24:29. What do these passages have in common?

_____

_____

In this portion of the Sermon, Jesus reveals that grace, love, and forgiveness can reverse the dangers of evil and retribution and create a new standard for community. Bonhoeffer (1979/1937) goes on to explain,

> The Church is not to be a national community like the old Israel, but a community of believers without political or national ties. The old Israel had been both - the chosen people of God *and* a national community, and it was therefore his will that they should meet force with force. But with the Church it is different: it has abandoned political and national status, and therefore it must patiently endure aggression. Otherwise, evil will be heaped upon evil. (p.141)

Read Isaiah 50:6-10 and describe the action and the expectation:

_____

_____

The next section of the Sermon dives deeper into the kind of love we are called to display. Just as elsewhere in the Sermon, Jesus is not content with our outward behavior (nonresistance to evil), He wants to have lordship over our hearts as well ("love your enemies"). This love does not excuse evil, but it recognizes the brokenness that evil displays. This love perceives that hearts strangled with hatred are to be pitied and cared for, not destroyed.

Does anyone in your life come to mind when you consider brokenness and evil through the lens of pity instead of hatred? Prayerfully consider this question, and prayerfully respond in your heart to the one(s) that God is bringing to mind. Note their names or initials here.

_____

_____

When viewed this way, it is easier to see why Jesus would ask us to bless those who persecute us, do good to them, and pray for them. All these actions could only be motivated by a true understanding of the nature of their motivations. It's easy to love those who treat us well. It's only Jesus' grace that allows us to love those who treat us poorly.

Read Luke 10:25-37 and summarize the message:

_____

_____

Read the following passages and describe the example of praying for our enemies:

Acts 7:60

_____

Luke 23:34

_____

The early church was commanded to the same response through persecution, even unto death.

Read the following passages and summarize the teaching:

Romans 12:14

_____

1 Corinthians 4:12-13

---

1 Thessalonians 5:15

The reward that Jesus promises in Matthew 5:45 is great: "that you may be children of your Father in heaven." In order to better understand how we are most fully honoring our Father in heaven, read 1 John 4:7-12.

What word is repeated in this passage? How many times?

In every interaction and teaching Jesus provided, the central theme is love. The call of discipleship is the abandonment of self-interest and adoption of the type of love God showed us through the person and work of Jesus Christ. We were His enemies, and He radically loved us.

But God shows His love for us in that while we were still sinners, Christ died for us. - Romans 5:8

Watch Study With Friends Video Series: The Sermon, Episode 5.5

WEEK SIX

KINGDOM RELIGION
(MATTHEW 6:1-24)

Beware of practicing your righteousness before other people in order to be seen by them, for then you will have no reward from your Father who is in heaven. [2] Thus, when you give to the needy, sound no trumpet before you, as the hypocrites do in the synagogues and in the streets, that they may be praised by others. Truly, I say to you, they have received their reward. [3] But when you give to the needy, do not let your left hand know what your right hand is doing, [4] so that your giving may be in secret. And your Father who sees in secret will reward you. [5] And when you pray, you must not be like the hypocrites. For they love to stand and pray in the synagogues and at the street corners, that they may be seen by others. Truly, I say to you, they have received their reward. [6] But when you pray, go into your room and shut the door and pray to your Father who is in secret. And your Father who sees in secret will reward you. [7] And when you pray, do not heap up empty phrases as the Gentiles do, for they think that they will be heard for their many words. [8] Do not be like them, for your Father knows what you need before you ask Him. [9] Pray then like this: Our Father in heaven, hallowed be your name. [10] Your kingdom come, your will be done, on earth as it is in heaven. [11] Give us this day our daily bread, [12] and forgive us our debts, as we also have forgiven our debtors. [13] And lead us not into temptation, but deliver us from evil. [14] For if you forgive others their trespasses, your heavenly Father will also forgive you, [15] but if you do not forgive others their trespasses, neither will your Father forgive your trespasses. [16] And when you fast, do not look gloomy like the

hypocrites, for they disfigure their faces that their fasting may be seen by others. Truly, I say to you, they have received their reward. ¹⁷ *But when you fast, anoint your head and wash your face,* ¹⁸ *that your fasting may not be seen by others but by your Father who is in secret. And your Father who sees in secret will reward you.* ¹⁹ *Do not lay up for yourselves treasures on earth, where moth and rust[e] destroy and where thieves break in and steal,* ²⁰ *but lay up for yourselves treasures in heaven, where neither moth nor rust destroys and where thieves do not break in and steal.* ²¹ *For where your treasure is, there your heart will be also.* ²² *The eye is the lamp of the body. So, if your eye is healthy, your whole body will be full of light,* ²³ *but if your eye is bad, your whole body will be full of darkness. If then the light in you is darkness, how great is the darkness!* ²⁴ *No one can serve two masters, for either he will hate the one and love the other, or he will be devoted to the one and despise the other. You cannot serve God and money.*
–Matthew 6:1-24

In week one, we noted that verse 6:8 sums up the message of the Sermon: "Do not be like them."

This week that verse echoes loudly throughout, as Jesus addresses both the religious hypocrites (6:2, 5) and those without religion (6:7) and calls us to kingdom conformity instead.

At the beginning of the Sermon, Jesus described the qualities of all Christians. He goes on to establish a clear understanding of the law and direction for how to behave as His disciples. Here, He continues to teach His followers what righteousness looks like in practice, emphasizing the importance of a sincere and genuine connection with God.

Jesus starts this segment with a warning: Beware. He knows how easy it would be for us to follow Him outwardly while reserving our true hearts and minds for ourselves. He reminds us that He wants our whole being, not just our outward actions.

In some circles, the word "religion" has taken on a negative meaning. But if the Christian religion is the "practicing of righteousness" described in 6:1, Jesus makes it clear in this passage that religion practiced authentically by His disciples is much deeper than merely what is seen on the surface.

> "Without revelation, religion sinks back into a pernicious superstition." -Herman Bavinck (1909, p. 169)

DAY ONE

GIVING

The passage on giving, 6:1-4, is the first in a trio of religious obligations that express our duty to God (prayer), others (giving), and ourselves (the self-discipline of fasting). All three sections follow the same pattern: vivid imagery of the wrong (conspicuous) way to fulfill these duties contrasted with the Christian (quiet) way, which results in the blessing of God who sees in secret.

Wait a minute. Back in verse 5:16, we heard a call to the very public shining of our light. Now we hear that we should be private. Is this a contradiction? No. In these passages, Jesus is addressing different sins. "It is our human cowardice which made Him say 'let your light shine before others', and our human vanity which made Him tell us to beware of practicing our righteousness in front of others" (Stott, 2020, p. 106). He is drawing a distinction between moral righteousness and religious righteousness, between deeds and devotions. He is reminding us to prioritize God's glory over our own in all circumstances.

Notice that Jesus says "when" instead of "if" you give. The duty of giving was commanded by the Law.

Read Leviticus 19:9–10 and Exodus 23:11. Summarize these laws:

_____

_____

There is an abundance of teaching in the Bible about care and compassion for the poor. Jesus clearly expects His disciples to be generous givers, but outward generosity is not enough. Just as He deepened our understanding of the law with His teaching on anger and adultery, He again concerns Himself with the motivation of our generosity.

Read John 5:44 and John 12:43. Who is being addressed and what behavior is being called out?

_____

_____

What are some ways we might be tempted to get honor from others by drawing attention to our giving?

_____

_____

We are clearly commanded to clarify our giving and our motivation for giving as we practice this act of worship to God.

In verse 6:3 Jesus uses an interesting expression: Do not let your left hand know what your right hand is doing. The idea behind this expression is that we are keeping a secret from ourselves. This expression doubles down on the motivation of our giving because it points out that we can be giving in secret from others but still feel internally self-righteous and self-congratulating. In this way, an act of mercy becomes an act of vanity. If we congratulate ourselves on our righteousness then, in fact, we are still seeking the approval of humans instead of God. Giving should be an act of self-forgetfulness. We are not to preen and gloat over righteousness, even inwardly. We are only to seek the approval of God.

Read the following passages and describe the command:

Philippians 2:3-4

_____

1 Corinthians 10:24

_____

A tricky part of Matthew 6:1-4 is the idea of "reward."

What are some things you think of when you consider "rewards?"

_____

_____

Again, it seems contradictory for Jesus to command selflessness for an action but promise a reward for that same action. Doesn't the hope for a reward constitute a selfish motivation? In order to understand this, we must first understand what is meant by reward. This is not like the reward given in a public ceremony, but the reward of intimacy with God when we are inside His will.

C.S. Lewis (1941/2001) explains:

> Indeed, if we consider the unblushing promises of reward and the staggering nature of the rewards promised in the Gospels, it would seem that Our Lord finds our desires, not too strong, but too weak. We are half-hearted creatures, fooling about with drink and sex and ambition when infinite joy is offered us, like an ignorant child who wants to go on making mud pies in a slum because he cannot imagine what is meant by the offer of a holiday at the sea. We are far too easily pleased.

> We must not be troubled by unbelievers when they say that this promise of reward makes the Christian life a mercenary affair. There are different kinds of rewards. There is the reward which has no natural connection with the things you do to earn it, and is quite foreign to the desires that ought to accompany those things. Money is not the natural reward of love; that is why we call a man mercenary if he marries a woman for the sake of her money. But marriage is the proper reward for a real lover, and he is not mercenary for desiring it...The proper rewards are not simply tacked on to the activity for which they are given, but are the activity itself in consummation.

The reward for our righteousness is intimacy with God. This reward is internal, not external; it is intangible, not material.

Read James 4:1–10 and correlate it to this passage of the sermon:

_____

_____

James speaks eloquently about the idea of rewards. First, He denounces the approval of others, calling it "friendship with the world" and reminding us that this type of friendship puts us in opposition to God. He goes on to say that when we draw closer to God (by following His commands) He draws closer to us (the reward, or natural outcome, for obedience).

Summarize 2 Corinthians 9:6-7:

Watch Study With Friends Video Series: The Sermon, Episode 6.1

DAY TWO

THE HEART OF PRAYER

In His second example of religious righteousness, verses 6:5-15, Jesus addresses prayer. This is a dense segment of the sermon, so we will give it two days of study. We see the same themes here that we discussed in the previous segment, so let's review them.

How does Jesus define righteousness and hypocrisy?

_____

_____

What is meant by earthly and heavenly rewards?

_____

_____

What people groups create the culture that Jesus calls Christians to reject?

_____

_____

There is no question that prayer is an important part of our relationship with God. The hypocrisy Jesus describes in these verses is a prayer for the sake of a societal reward, accolades from peers, or pride in oneself. In the same way that giving to the needy can become an act of vanity when done for self-righteous reasons, so can the act of attending church or praying publicly. Having the wrong mindset and heart-set destroys the righteousness of the act.

Read Daniel 6:10. Where did Daniel pray? How many times a day?

What are some ways that prayer can become filled with hypocrisy (v.5) or empty phrases (v. 7) in church or bible studies?

On the other hand, there is incredible intimacy with God when we come to Him in humble prayer. We can have peace and surrender on a scale that surpasses human understanding when we take a posture of prayer that recognizes God for who He is.

In verse six, Jesus uses an expression that is worth noting. He says, "Go into your room and shut the door." Clearly, the shutting of the door reminds us to remove distractions and the prying eyes of others (we have all peeked at others during prayer time, let's be honest). There is also a sense that God is waiting for us in this quiet place. He initiates conversation through His many revelations of Himself: His Son, His Word, and all of Creation. We come to our time of prayer in response to Him.

Interestingly, the Greek word for the room where we are to go for prayer is *tameion* which can also be used to describe a storage room where treasures or provisions might be kept. The significance of that word, then, is that we enter the prayer room with the confidence of finding treasures and provisions. Fully absorbing that meaning may change our approach to prayer from obligatory to expectational.

Read Matthew 16:18-19. Do you see a parallel to the notion of a storeroom here? Hint: what do the "keys" open?

This confident expectation is reiterated in verse 8: "for your Father knows what you need before you ask Him."

Read Isaiah 65:24 and note the parallel to this portion of the Sermon:

Jesus is not discouraging us from making petitions to God. Rather, He is explaining that we should not try to ply Him with our pleas. He already knows what is best for us. As Bonhoeffer describes, "Our prayer can never be an entreaty to God, for we have no need to come before Him in that way. We are privileged to know that He knows our needs before we ask Him. This is what gives Christian prayer its boundless confidence and its joyous certainty" (Bonhoeffer, 1979/1937, p. 163).

Read the following passages and describe the rewards of humble, heartfelt prayer:

Romans 8:15–16

Hebrews 4:14–16

Prayer is meant to be highly relational. Jesus describes our proper posture in prayer and warns us against hypocrisy in prayer, but He also uses "Father" language to emphasize the relational.

What does 1 Thessalonians 5:16–18 say about prayer?

Do you have a close friend or family member with whom you speak several times a day? Is there someone who is the first call you make when something significant occurs in your life?

My husband and I have two daughters, now in college over 700 miles away from where we live. As a result of the distance, we must be very intentional about connecting with them. I worried about this when they were leaving but it turns out that the relationship we had built before they left laid a foundation for what we have now. We talk to each other several times a day. Thanks to group FaceTime we often talk all four together. They call us between classes, they call us from Target (ok, to be fair that's usually a budget negotiation), they call us for advice, or to share in some joyful moment. They call when they are bored. They tell us about their day, they ask about our day. I am grateful for this level of relationship with them.

Let me be plain about the connection to prayer that I am making with this analogy: When circumstances changed (the physical distance) and made the relationship more difficult, there turned out to be a clear benefit that resulted from us building a foundation of good communication before that difficult time happened.

Take the analogy further. These conversations with the girls are not always transactional from an ask/answer point of view. Sometimes when they call, we don't get a resolution. They have problems that can't be worked out immediately. Not everything should be fixed or solved by Mom and Dad. But we are doing life together: ups and downs, good and bad. We are in a relationship.

That's what this teaching is about. God is calling us into such an intimate relationship with Him that He would be our first 'call.' He desires that we would be talking to Him and listening to Him all day long about the big and little things. A lot goes on in a day! But with this ongoing conversation in mind, it's easier to understand how we can pray without ceasing. The truth is that we are in the presence of God all the time - we might as well be talking to Him and listening to Him.

The last bit of that 1 Thessalonians 5:16-18 passage also reiterates the gospel: for this is the will of God in Christ Jesus for you. The person and work of Christ is completely tied to the relationship with the Father to whom He gives us access. By regularly responding to God's grace and mercy through heartfelt prayer, we receive the reward of His presence, guidance, and comfort in our daily lives.

Watch Study With Friends Video Series: The Sermon, Episode 6.2

DAY THREE

CHRISTIAN PRAYER

On day two of this week's study, we focused on the imperative of genuine, heartfelt prayer. Now we ask: can a prayer that is memorized and repeated weekly (or daily) be genuinely heartfelt? Is there a conflict between heartfelt and memorized prayer? How do we consider the repetition many of us have experienced around these verses, now called "The Lord's Prayer," in our own church and personal life?

What are your initial thoughts on the potential benefits and challenges of memorized prayer?

_____

_____

In Matthew's account, Jesus teaches these verses as a guide for prayer, saying "Pray then like this" (v.9). In Luke's account, Jesus provides the prayer itself saying "When you pray, say..." (Luke 11:2). Both interpretations are suitable for use as the foundation for Christian prayer. Whether we recite the prayer or use it as a model for our prayers, we receive the instruction Jesus gave.

Do you utilize these scriptures in your personal or corporate church prayer time? If so, how?

_____

The model of the Lord's Prayer closely reflects the proper approach to God found in the model of the Old Testament Tabernacle. Notice the common elements listed below.

Obedience and submission to God's government/kingdom as the first order of approaching Him:

"Our Father in heaven, hallowed be your name. Your kingdom come, your will be done, on earth as it is in heaven."

Bringing an offering to the gate of the Tabernacle showed submission to the government and Kingdom of God and obedience to Him as the King of kings.

Acknowledgment of the need for self-reflection, forgiveness, and reconciliation:

"Forgive us our debts, as we forgive our debtors." (emphasized in vv. 14-15)	In the courtyard of the Tabernacle, the altar of burnt offerings is for repentance and reconciliation. The laver is for cleansing and self-examination.

The presence and provision of God through the intimacy of a shared meal:

"Give us this day our daily bread"	The table of showbread in the Tabernacle symbolizes God's provision for Israel and highlights the intimate fellowship that exists between God and His people.

A prayer for deliverance and safekeeping:

"And lead us not into temptation, but deliver us from evil."	The altar of incense in the Tabernacle symbolizes the prayers of God's people

By praying the Lord's Prayer, we enter into fellowship with Him. Through the progressive actions required to enter the Tabernacle, the nation of Israel was represented before the "Holy of Holies" where God's presence dwelled.

Are there any other elements shared by the Lord's Prayer and the Tabernacle?

_____

_____

How do these parallels deepen our understanding of the Lord's Prayer?

_____

_____

By instructing us to begin prayer with "Our Father in heaven," Jesus reminds us of two important things: God is both very personal (our Father) and He is divine (in heaven). It is always wise to set our minds on these parallel truths so that we might rightly position ourselves in grateful humility as we pray.

Read 1 John 3:1a and note your reflections on how God sees us:

_____

This awareness of God as personal and divine sets the tone for all prayer: As the divine, God is the priority (your name, your kingdom, your will be done). As our Father, He cares deeply about us and we can surrender our needs to Him (give us, forgive us, deliver us).

Seeing the Lord's Prayer through this dual lens brings to mind the dual nature of the Ten Commandments. The first four commandments prioritize our glorification and honor of God. Commandments 5-10 deal with our human interactions.

Take a moment to reflect on all the ways the Sermon relates so tightly to the rest of scripture. What kind of encouragement does that give you?

_____

_____

There is a prayer embedded in the prayer here. Alongside the important elements of worship of God and acceptance of His provision, there is a phrase that deserves some examination: "lead us not into temptation, but deliver us from evil."

Read James 1:13. Does this passage seem to conflict with the first part of the phrase above? If so, how?

_____

_____

God never entices us to sin, but He does allow tests of our faith and character. Stott explains, "it is the devil who is in view, who tempts God's people to sin, and from whom we need to be rescued" (Stott, 2020, p. 127).

Read James 1:2 and paraphrase it here:

_____

_____

If we are to count it all joy when we meet trials of various kinds, how are we also justified in asking to be "delivered from evil" and the trials that come with it? The answer may be that we pray not to be spared from these temptations and trials, but that we might be given the strength to overcome them. Stott suggests a good paraphrase might be "Do not allow us so to be led into temptation that it overwhelms us but rescue us from the evil one" (Stott, 2020).

Read 1 Corinthians 10:13 and describe how it intertwines with this phrase in the Lord's Prayer:

_____

_____

As much as we all want to grip tightly to a fresh interaction with God each time we pray, if we recite the Lord's Prayer regularly it can become more habitual than heartfelt. In the following section, use the above parallels and insights to rephrase the Lord's Prayer or summarize a personal articulation. This exercise is for you, so do it in a way that will stick with you the next time you recite the Lord's Prayer (or use it as the model for prayer). Recall the elements of the Tabernacle if they help you visualize your approach to the most holy God.

Our Father   _____

in heaven   _____

hallowed be your name.   _____

Your kingdom come   _____

your will be done, on earth as it is in heaven.   _____

Give us this day our daily bread   _____

and forgive us our debts, as we also have forgiven   _____
our debtors.

And lead us not into temptation, but deliver us   _____
from evil.

Watch Study With Friends Video Series: The Sermon, Episode 6.3

DAY FOUR

FASTING

In verses 6:16-18 we return to the themes discussed when we studied verses 6:1-8. Since Jesus repeated these themes three times, let's follow His lead by drilling them in once again.

How does Jesus define righteousness and hypocrisy?

_____

_____

What is meant by earthly and heavenly rewards?

_____

_____

What people groups create the culture that Jesus calls Christians to reject?

_____

_____

The Pharisees fasted twice a week on Mondays and Thursdays (Luke 18:12). John the Baptist and his disciples fasted, but the disciples of Jesus did not (Matthew 9:14, Luke 5:33). Jesus explains this distinction in Matthew 9:15, "Can the wedding guests mourn as long as the bridegroom is with them? The days will come when the bridegroom is taken away from them, and then they will fast." Here in the Sermon, there is an expectation that Jesus' disciples will fast, and it is a reiteration of Old Testament law.

Like with giving and prayer, Jesus cares about our motivation for fasting. It should not be self-centered in any way.

What are some ways fasting can become self-centered instead of God-centered?

Biblical fasting is clearly abstaining from food. Abstaining from other activities can also have value, but biblically, the voluntary experience of discomfort through hunger is the definition of fasting. This discomfort *connects our spiritual life to our physical life*, creating a holistic experience that deepens our intimacy with God. Scot McKnight explains, "Fasting in the Bible is the organic unified response of a whole person to a sacred moment. We can provoke more Biblical fasting simply by teaching a more organic sense of who we are" (McKnight, 2013, p. 201).

Read the following passages and note your own view on the spiritual connectedness of our bodies and souls:

1 Thessalonians 5:23

---

1 Corinthians 6:19–20

The stationary fast (i.e., always on a particular day or days of the week) can be useful but, like reciting the Lord's Prayer, it can also become hollow if we are not careful to intentionally orient our hearts and minds toward righteousness. There are three biblical foundations for fasting: special prayer, self-discipline, and mercy for/solidarity with the poor.

Special prayer can be rooted in repentance or petition, but in any case, there is a heightened awareness of the need for God's intervention. Biblical examples can be found in Nehemiah 9:1-2, Jonah 3:5, Esther 4:12-17, and Daniel 9:1-19.

Choose one or two of the scriptures above and reflect on the special prayer that is coupled with fasting:

Modern examples for the corporate body (the church) to call for prayer with fasting might be the devastation from a natural disaster, a mass shooting, or the threat of war. Personal reasons to pray and fast might be a troubled family member, a significant career change, or discernment over a ministry calling. There is also a warrant for prayer and fasting when we become aware of a particularly stubborn sin in our lives and the need for God to intervene with mercy and grace so that we can turn from that sin. Here, examples might be a persistent struggle with pornography, pride, anger, etc.

Self-discipline is also in view when we undertake the practice of fasting. Much of our sin originates in our bodies, so the regular practice of disciplining those desires is quite useful.

Read Galatians 5:16-17, 22-23 and note the connection to the self-discipline of fasting:

_____

_____

As Bonhoeffer describes, "It is always true of the disciple that the spirit is willing, but the flesh is weak, and he must therefore 'watch and pray.' The spirit knows the right way and desires to follow it, but the flesh lacks the courage and finds it too hard, too hazardous and wearisome, and so it stifles the voice of the spirit...we have to practice the strictest daily discipline; only so can the flesh learn the painful lesson that it has no rights of its own" (Bonhoeffer, 1979/1937, p. 170).

Read 1 Corinthians 9:24-27 and note the connection between fasting and self-discipline:

_____

Voluntarily becoming physically uncomfortable and overcoming that discomfort for our spiritual growth is an important element in the practice of fasting. Regularly conquering a basic fleshly desire trains us and strengthens us for the life God calls us to live.

If fasting is rarely practiced in the Christian life, then fasting to show mercy for the poor is even more rarely practiced. However, God is very clear in His intent about this.

Read and summarize Isaiah 58:1-14:

_____

_____

The command here is clear: regular fasting so that we can share what we might have eaten (or the cost) with the poor and poorly nourished. Even if we regularly contribute to hunger charities, this intent can fade into the background, especially if we have set up hands-off monthly deductions from a bank account. Directing our fasting practice toward the poor keeps this population at the top of our prayers and actions, the way that God intended.

As we wrap up today's study, take a moment to consider how you might incorporate fasting into your spiritual practices (if you do not already do so):

- Are there special prayers or personal sins on which you can focus?
- Are there world events that are grieving you?
- Can you invite self-discipline into your life in a new way?
- Might a stationary (regularly scheduled) fast help you to have more resources to dedicate to the poor and underfed in your community?

Fasting is mentioned in the Bible more than 70 times. Taking God's word seriously in this spiritual practice is a blessing…and a command.

For teenagers, young adults, or anyone who struggles with body image, fasting may not be appropriate. Please consult with your counselor to uncover whether this spiritual practice is healthy for you. For additional resources on this, see Appendix B.

Watch Study With Friends Video Series: The Sermon, Episode 6.4

DAY FIVE

TREASURE

The first portion of Matthew 6 focused on the private Christian life. In verses 6:19-24 Jesus shifts focus to our public business with the world by addressing money, possessions, food, drink, and clothing. Some might distinguish these into "religious" and "secular" activities, but Jesus teaches us that everything we do should be done with an awareness of God's will, presence, and provision. This is exactly the point: God is equally concerned with all areas of our life.

Refresh your memory of the phrase that sums up the entire Sermon by writing the first five words of 6:8 (ESV):

_____

In verses 6:1-4 Jesus warns against being generous with our money for a public display of piety, like the Pharisees. Here in 6:19-24, He deepens the teaching by warning against being like the non-religious whose culture focuses on materialism. He aids in our understanding by providing contrasts: treasures in earth or heaven, living in light or darkness, prioritizing God or money. Each section (19-21, 22-23, 24) is structured the same: a statement, two observations, and a conclusion. But in every case the message is clear: do not be like them. Jesus calls His disciples to detach from goods and wealth. We sometimes call these things our "resources."

Write your own definition of "resource," then compare/contrast worldly vs. spiritual resources:

_____

_____

_____

In verses 19-20, Jesus redefines security. Many people find security in money because it can purchase the things they need and want. Jesus reminds us that worldly treasures are fleeting, but real security is found in heaven. Nothing we acquire on earth can be held after death. As Job says in 1:21, "Naked I came from my mother's womb, and naked shall I return." Job exemplifies the proper perspective on God and material possessions in the second part of that verse: "The Lord gave, and the Lord has taken away; blessed be the name of the Lord."

Rephrase the Job passage in your own words:

_____

_____

This message does not prohibit possessions or being wise about planning for the future. In fact, in Proverbs 6:6-11 and 1 Timothy 5:8 we are cautioned not to be lazy about working hard to provide for ourselves and our families.

Read Proverbs 6:6–11 and 1 Timothy 5:8 and summarize them:

_____

_____

Considering the above, what are some healthy ways to balance God's provision and our own provision for ourselves and our families?

_____

_____

Matthew 6:19-20 is also not in conflict with 1 Timothy 4:4 which reminds us that God has given us good gifts to enjoy. But, like elsewhere in the Sermon, we are called to correct prioritization: God first, everything else second.

Notice the verse says "Do not store up for yourselves…" which cuts to the heart of why we store up: selfishness. Storing up treasures greedily and being blind to the needs of others is the opposite of Christian charity.

According to the 2022 World Bank *Poverty and Prosperity Report*, almost a quarter of the global population, 23 percent (about 1.8 billion), lives on less than $3.65 per day, and almost half, 47 percent (about 3.7 billion), lives on less than $6.85 per day (World Bank, 2022). Sit with those figures for a moment.

Reflect on the people experiencing homelessness or food insecurity in your area. Now think about your own situation. Can you sacrifice more? Can you give more to others? What are some common reasons people provide for not giving to others?

_____

_____

Read James 5:2–5. Compare it to Matthew 6:19–21 and write your reflections:

_____

_____

Read 1 Corinthians 13:13 and list the things that "abide."

_____

Jesus calls us to live a life on earth that is constantly aware of the life to come. That message continues in verses 22-23 when He declares the "eye is the lamp of the body." In this short passage, Jesus uses the metaphor of light and darkness for good and evil. This reminds us of when He did so earlier in the Sermon.

Write your own summary of Matthew 5:14-15 from earlier in the study:

_____

The heart and eye are often biblically interchangeable, so 'set your heart' and 'fix your eye' have the same intent.

Read and summarize Deuteronomy 15:9:

_____

_____

If verses 19-21 emphasize having our heart in the right place, verses 22-23 emphasize having our eyes on the right thing. In the same way that the healthy physical eye guides us properly, so does the healthy spiritual eye guide us into God's will, especially regarding our treasures. Scot McKnight (2013) notes:

> The words used for "healthy" (haplous) and "unhealthy" (poneros) are words often used for "generous" and "stingy." Words that appear to be rather innocent take on a more pointed economic flavor. The economic hints of these images make clearer why "healthy" and "unhealthy" are connected to the previous [passage] ("treasure" in 6:21) and the following one ("God and money" in 6:24): the image about the lamp and the eye is a moral image for how one responds to the needy with compassion. (p. 208)

Read Proverbs 22:9 and summarize it:

_____

_____

Wherever we focus our attention (or fix our eye) will certainly guide us. If our ambition is self-glory, that will guide our actions, especially how we view and manage our treasures. Conversely, if our ambition is God's glory, our treasures of time, money, and other resources will be directed toward Him and His kingdom.

Where would you say most of your ambition is, based on the amount of time you give it each day?

_____

_____

This ambition is the focus of the final verse, 6:24. By using "master" language, Jesus recalls the first commandment regarding serving idols and relates it to possessions. His audience would have readily understood the relationship between this and Deuteronomy 6:4: there is only one God. This is a perfect punctuation mark on the previous passages which boil down to worship and idolatry.

Read and rephrase James 4:4:

_____

_____

Jesus knows the strangely acute pull of comfort in material things. McKnight (2013) calls possessions "mysteriously idolatrous" (p. 205). Jesus warns in this passage that we must wrestle daily with our hearts and minds to worship God alone.

Watch Study With Friends Video Series: The Sermon, Episode 6.5

WEEK SEVEN

KINGDOM CHOICES
(MATTHEW 6:25-7:12)

[25]Therefore I tell you, do not be anxious about your life, what you will eat or what you will drink, nor about your body, what you will put on. Is not life more than food, and the body more than clothing? [26]Look at the birds of the air: they neither sow nor reap nor gather into barns, and yet your heavenly Father feeds them. Are you not of more value than they? [27]And which of you by being anxious can add a single hour to his span of life? [28]And why are you anxious about clothing? Consider the lilies of the field, how they grow: they neither toil nor spin, [29]yet I tell you, even Solomon in all his glory was not arrayed like one of these. [30]But if God so clothes the grass of the field, which today is alive and tomorrow is thrown into the oven, will he not much more clothe you, O you of little faith? [31]Therefore do not be anxious, saying, 'What shall we eat?' or 'What shall we drink?' or 'What shall we wear?' [32]For the Gentiles seek after all these things, and your heavenly Father knows that you need them all. [33]But seek first the kingdom of God and his righteousness, and all these things will be added to you. [34]Therefore do not be anxious about tomorrow, for tomorrow will be anxious for itself. Sufficient for the day is its own trouble. [1]Judge not, that you be not judged. [2]For with the judgment you pronounce you will be judged, and with the measure you use it will be measured to you. [3]Why do you see the speck that is in your brother's eye, but do not notice the log that is in your own eye? [4]Or how can you say to your brother, 'Let me take the speck out of your eye,' when there is the log in your own eye? [5]You hypocrite, first take the log out of your own eye,

and then you will see clearly to take the speck out of your brother's eye. 6Do not give dogs what is holy, and do not throw your pearls before pigs, lest they trample them underfoot and turn to attack you. 7Ask, and it will be given to you; seek, and you will find; knock, and it will be opened to you. 8For everyone who asks receives, and the one who seeks finds, and to the one who knocks it will be opened. 9Or which one of you, if his son asks him for bread, will give him a stone? 10Or if he asks for a fish, will give him a serpent? 11If you then, who are evil, know how to give good gifts to your children, how much more will your Father who is in heaven give good things to those who ask him! 12So whatever you wish that others would do to you, do also to them, for this is the Law and the Prophets.
–Matthew 6:25–7:12

In Matthew 6:25-7:12, Jesus presents instructions on worrying about material things, prioritizing grace over condemnation, choosing wise speech over foolish words, dependence on God through prayer over selfish independence, and embracing kindness over cruelty. Again, we hear the echo of 6:8, "Do not be like them." Each teaching highlights a choice between two ways of life: following the world or honoring the kingdom of God.

The world's ways are characterized by the pursuit of material possessions and the elevation of self. The world teaches us that our worth is measured by what we own and what we accomplish. The kingdom of God, on the other hand, is characterized by trust in God's provision, love for others, and the pursuit of righteousness. The kingdom of God teaches us that our worth is measured by our relationship with God and our love for others.

In this portion of the Sermon, Jesus presents His disciples with yet another challenge to examine our lives and to make a conscious choice to follow the ways of the kingdom of God.

DAY ONE

CHOOSE PEACE

"Anxiety does not empty tomorrow of its sorrows, but only empties today of its strength."
- Charles Spurgeon (1889. p. 62)

In Matthew 6:25-34, Jesus points out the contradiction between faith and anxiety. At the risk of an abrupt start to this day of study, let's dive first into the issue this might seem to present for those who have a diagnosed anxiety disorder.

According to the National Institute of Mental Health, Generalized Anxiety Disorder (GAD) affects 6.8 million adults or 3.1% of the U.S. population" (Kessler, 2005, pp. 593-602). That means that there will be many who participate in this study (and even more who read these verses) who may feel conflicted in the area of faith and anxiety. To help us, we turn to James, pastor of the church in Jerusalem. He had a deep love for his people and for God. His people were suffering in horrible and difficult ways, yet he wrote:

²Count it all joy, my brothers, when you meet trials of various kinds, ³for you know that the testing of your faith produces steadfastness. ⁴And let steadfastness have its full effect, that you may be perfect and complete, lacking in nothing. – James 1:2–4

The suffering that results from "trials of various kinds" includes physical and mental challenges as well as the persecution James was directly referencing. Those who suffer, suffer.

List some ways that you commonly see suffering in your life or the broader culture:

_____

_____

The catalysts for suffering are too many to list, but this passage speaks to all of them. While God can and does miraculously heal illnesses of all kinds on occasion, in no case are we ever called to heal ourselves by faith: miracles are entirely up to God's discretion. That is true for both physical and mental health challenges. However, God remedies all suffering through Jesus.

Isaiah prophesied about Christ, saying that "with His wounds, we are healed" (53:5). This prophecy has an "already and not yet" implication for disciples of Jesus: we are already healed by the blood of Jesus which sustains us in this life, and we are not yet completely healed (as we will be when we live with Him in heaven).

Read Matthew 11:28–30 and reflect on this passage in the context of suffering:

_____

_____

Do you or someone in your life struggle with diagnosed anxiety? How might the James and Matthew passages above offer comfort and guidance?

_____

_____

We have seen one point made clear throughout the Sermon: While we are certainly called to outward discipleship, God is not concerned with what we can do, He is concerned with who we are in Christ. This holds true for anyone with a diagnosed disability. For more resources on disability theology, see Appendix B.

There is a difference between diagnosed anxiety disorders and anxiety that is a result of relying more on ourselves than on God. In these verses, Jesus is speaking directly to His disciples, with the assumption that we believe God is sovereign. Mental health issues notwithstanding, He is pointing out that the contradiction between faith and anxiety is our *choice*.

Read 1 Corinthians 8:6 and paraphrase it into your own belief statement.

_____

_____

Despite this confession of faith, many of us don't live our daily lives as if we believe it. Because Jesus starts this section of the Sermon with the word "therefore," He is drawing our attention to the teaching leading up to it. That section is about material things. Do we believe that our treasures create our security, or that God does? Jesus is imploring us to remember that since God is our Creator, responsible for sustaining us in every way, we must believe that the presence or absence of provisions is in His hands, not ours.

Considering this truth, we must also accept that faith and provision are not a one-to-one correlation.

Read the following passages and note the complexities of how provision interacts with God's sovereign will by answering the three questions indicated:

Job 1:6-12

What is happening?	Who is faithful but still suffering?	Why is the faithful suffering?

Jeremiah 29:10

What is happening?	Who is faithful but still suffering?	Why is the faithful suffering?

Amos 8:4-6

What is happening?	Who is faithful but still suffering?	Why is the faithful suffering?

While there are nuances to the responses in the third column, like testing, corrupt leaders, or the powerful exploiting the poor, an appropriate answer in all rows of column three would have been "It was part of God's plan." Those who teach that if we believe hard enough, we will be guaranteed anything (material wealth, or lack of suffering in particular) are way off base. They twist Matthew 6:33 into a horrible perversion. Our lives exist for God's glory alone and it is up to Him how He chooses to use them. But in any case, we are not in control, He is.

Read and summarize James 4:13-14:

_____

_____

Jesus teaches us that freedom is found in recognizing that we belong to God alone and, as a result, relinquishing the desire to control our own lives. In Matthew 6:25-33, He uses two illustrations: the birds of the air and the flowers of the field, neither of which has a car, fancy clothes, or any "collectibles." The freedom we are offered is the kind of existence that is utterly dependent upon Him, not at all dependent upon material things.

Once we give up the idea of control, we can experience peace. When we are consumed by control (or lack of it) we experience chaos, unrest, dissension, depression, and distress of all sorts (like those without faith, referenced in verse 6:32). When we seek His kingdom first (think, Beatitudes), we will be given what our loving Father knows we need. No, that might not always look the way we wish it would. But we choose Him anyway, because He first chose us, bled for us, died for us, and offered us resurrection life in Himself.

The verses from earlier in today's study, then, converge on both types of anxiety.

Read James 1:2-4 and Matthew 11:28-30 again. Synthesize them, in the full context of the gospel, into your understanding about worry over material things:

_____

_____

Use the first column below to list things you want to control and in the corresponding space, write a prayer of surrender to God.

Control	Surrender

Watch Study With Friends Video Series: The Sermon, Episode 7.1

DAY TWO

CHOOSE GRACE

In Matthew 7:1-5, Jesus defines the difference between grace and condemnation, providing us with a hard look at ourselves. He reminds us that our imperfections are large and looming over our own lives, and we would be better served to focus on them instead of the faults of others.

Imagine the most disorganized, clutter-filled, rat-infested home. Now picture that homeowner taking a walk around the block criticizing the length of grass in each of his neighbors' perfectly-manicured lawns.

What are some ways we judge each other in everyday life? Are there any ways you have felt judged?

_____

_____

Because of the term judgment used here, this passage is sometimes misunderstood. Let's look at a few questions that have been historically raised about this passage.

Does this passage mean Jesus is against judges and courts?

No. Those human institutions were put in place by God for the purpose of judging good from evil and bringing punishment where appropriate.

Read Romans 13:1-5, and 1 Peter 2:13-17 and summarize the biblical view of these institutions:

_____

_____

Does this passage mean we should never judge another person's actions?

No. All over the bible, God calls us to be wise in discerning peoples' hearts by their actions.

Read and summarize 1 John 4:1-6.

_____

_____

Further evidence that we are to be wise in our judgment of those around us immediately follows this passage. In 7:6 we are warned how to judge people to inform us on when/where to speak, and the main points in 7:15-27 equip us to identify the wise and foolish around us. Clearly, there is an important call to understand how to accurately judge others.

What, then, should we learn from this passage? Not surprisingly, the best interpretation of this passage is a reiteration of the entire Sermon: we should remember grace when looking upon others, be aware of our own sinful state and need for God's mercy, and not withhold that kind of mercy from those around us. We should focus on our own sin and seek sanctification before we point out someone else's downfalls. The parallel passage from Luke offers a good visual. In Luke 6:39 Jesus asks, "Can a blind man lead a blind man? Will they not both fall into a pit?"

Read John 8:1-7 and note how it interacts with Matthew 7:1-5.

_____

_____

Furthermore, Jesus warns that if we wrongly place ourselves in the judgment seat, we cannot then plead ignorance of the law we "oversee."

Read James 4:11-12 and Romans 2:1-3 and note the phrasing of judging and being judged.

_____

_____

Removal of the "speck" holds a special kind of hypocrisy: an act of apparent kindness is actually designed to elevate ourselves. Rather, a supporting passage in Romans advises the opposite:

Summarize Romans 14:1-13.

You may be wondering how this passage intersects with 1 Corinthians 5, particularly verses 12-13: "For what have I to do with judging outsiders? Is it not those inside the church whom you are to judge? God judges those outside. 'Purge the evil person from among you.'"

Rather than contradicting, these two passages complement one another. Together, they speak to the importance of both personal responsibility and corporate accountability in the Christian life. Matthew 7:1-5 teaches us not to judge others in a way that is hypocritical or unloving. Instead, we should be patient and merciful, seeking to help others with compassion and grace. 1 Corinthians 5:12-13, on the other hand, reminds us of the importance of corporate accountability within the church. It is the responsibility of the church to discipline its own members and to maintain the purity of the church community. This means that we must hold one another accountable for our actions and seek to address sin within the church.

These passages are not in conflict but must both be understood in their proper context to see the harmony they have with each other: be cautious when judging at all, but maintain the high standard Jesus sets, here in the Sermon and elsewhere, for His disciples. In every case, we are to judge with humility, love, and grace.

To summarize the Sermon's instruction on judgment, consider the words of John Stott (2020) in the context of how the culture sees Christians:

> In a word, [Jesus is prohibiting] 'censoriousness.' [This type of judgment] does not mean to assess people critically, but to judge them harshly. A censorious critic is a fault-finder who is negative and destructive towards other people and enjoys actively seeking out their failings. Such a person puts the worst possible construction on the motives of others, pours cold water on their schemes and is ungenerous towards their mistakes. (p. 150)

124

Prayerfully consider if there are people or situations you have wrongly judged. Note them here as a way of staying accountable for fixing any damage you may have caused.

Watch Study With Friends Video Series: The Sermon, Episode 7.2

DAY THREE

CHOOSE WISE SPEECH

Matthew 7:6 contains rough language that may seem foreign in the context of the Sermon, but remember, this is the same Jesus who called the Pharisees "whitewashed tombs" and "a brood of vipers." He is not afraid to speak truthfully and harshly when needed.

Why do you think Jesus may have occasionally used severe language?

So why does He speak so strongly here? What exactly is this analogy intended to teach us?

Notice the clear division in this verse between the common and the sacred. The visuals Jesus used would have been easily understood by the original audience because they were more commonly used during that time. For example, the note on dogs tearing up the sacred would likely have been referencing the Gentiles, since dogs are also used elsewhere to describe them (Matthew 15:26-27, Philippians 3:2, Revelation 22:15). Also, Jesus uses the word pearl elsewhere to refer to the kingdom of God (Matthew 13:45-46). An accurate interpretation would be "Do not [yet] bring the gospel to the Gentiles, the Jews come first."

This interpretation is supported by Acts 13:46 and Acts 18:5-6. Read those passages and summarize Paul's sentiment.

However, this contextual truth makes the passage tricky to interpret because we later read Jesus's words, "But you will receive power when the Holy Spirit has come upon you, and you will be my witnesses in Jerusalem and in all Judea and Samaria, and to the end of the earth." (Acts 1:8)

To affirm our gospel directive, read and summarize Mark 16:15 and 2 Corinthians 2:14–17.

_____

_____

Clearly, we are called to present the gospel to all. Is the instruction about not offering the sacred (the gospel/kingdom of God) to dogs and swine, then, no longer useful? Is it bound to the time when Jesus said it (prior to the Great Commission, the Resurrection, and the entire book of Acts)? On the contrary. There are three ways we can use this verse instructively in our own lives.

First, some in the early church thought the "sacred" was in reference to Communion, with a prohibition against allowing non-believers to partake. This is certainly true, but not the full extent of the meaning of the passage.

The second application of the passage is a call to start our gospel work with those closest to us. In this way, we follow the model of Jesus, the disciples, and the early church who started close to home and worked their way outward into the world.

But, perhaps most accurately, we should see this verse as a warning. While we are certainly called to share the gospel with everyone, there will be some who remain hard-hearted. These, Calvin says, are the dogs and swine in our lives:

> It ought to be understood, that *dogs* and *swine* are names given not to every kind of debauched men, or to those who are destitute of the fear of God and of true godliness, but to those who, by clear evidences, have manifested a hardened contempt of God, so that their disease appears to be incurable. In another passage, Christ places the *dogs* in contrast with the elect people of God and the household of faith. It *is not proper to take the children's bread, and give it to dogs,* (Matthew 15:26.) But by *dogs* and *swine* he means here those who are so thoroughly imbued with a wicked contempt of God, that they refuse to accept any remedy. (Calvin, 1555/1846)

Calvin's interpretation is supported by Jesus' words when he sent out the twelve. Read the entirety of Matthew 10 and note the connection between Matthew 10:14 and Matthew 7:6.

_____

_____

Not everyone will be interested in kingdom living, but this is a measure of the wise and the fool.

Read and paraphrase Proverbs 9:8.

_____

Can you think of people in your life that have closed their hearts to the gospel? Is there any time that you can recall when speaking up about the gospel invited ridicule or rancor? In retrospect, would you do anything differently?

_____

_____

_____

Speak about the gospel with care. Treasure it and convey it to others with the wise and winsome speech that honors God. In this way, we honor Christ and present ourselves as true gospel carriers.

Watch Study With Friends Video Series: The Sermon, Episode 7.3

DAY FOUR

CHOOSE PRAYER

In verses 7:7-11 we return to the matter of prayer, but from a slightly different angle than we viewed the practice in verses 6:5-15. Here, Jesus gives us the command to ask, seek, and knock. He offers a promise that God is accessible through these actions and that our prayers will be heard. He reminds us of our relationship with God by again using "Father" language, deepening the instruction with human examples of parent/child requests and relationships.

Earlier in the Sermon (6:6), Jesus instructs. "When you pray, go into your room and shut the door and pray to your Father who is in secret." This room (some translate closet) has some different meanings that are useful as we consider the intimacy and power of petitionary prayer. The room or chamber described here could mean the place where our greatest treasures are stored, which reminds us that our relationship with God is our greatest treasure. The closet reminds us that we enter here to shed our clothing (become naked/vulnerable in prayer) and put on new clothing (emerging changed from our time of intimacy with the Lord). Trusting that the prayer experience will be transformational, let's consider the two parts of this passage: our petitions and God's goodness.

When it comes to the petitions we bring to God, we may note that in verses 7-8, Jesus uses three descriptions of our requests: ask, seek, and knock. Is this passage teaching persistence in prayer? If so, that would be supported elsewhere.

Read Luke 11:5-8 and Luke 18:1-8. What is the result of the persistence displayed here?

_____

_____

But what is meant by persistence? Do we need to rouse God from distraction or sleep to act on our behalf? Do we need to remind Him what we asked for last week? Of course not. Rather, this exhortation of persistence reminds us that we are prone to distraction and laziness ourselves.

By making prayer a consistent practice we stay aware of our dependence on God and we stay involved in the intimate relationship He offers.

This passage also teaches us that our prayers will be heard. Since we have access to the Father through Christ, we should regularly engage that relationship with great gratitude, among a host of other mindsets.

Read Ephesians 3:11-12. Write the two descriptive words about how we should approach God.

_____

Are there times you feel less bold or confident in approaching God? If so, why?

_____

_____

The entire book of Psalm is a prayer book. Petitionary prayer (asking for what we need) is taught all over the Bible. All of this points to the assurance that God is listening attentively to us.

Read the following verses and make their truths personal by rephrasing them in a statement about your own relationship with God:

Proverbs 8:17

_____

Jeremiah 29:13-14

_____

James 1:5, 17

_____

We have said multiple times in this study that the Book of James closely parallels the Sermon. James 4:2-3 deepens our understanding of petitionary prayers: "²You desire and do not have, so you murder. You covet and cannot obtain, so you fight and quarrel. You do not have, because you do not ask. ³You ask and do not receive, because you ask wrongly, to spend it on your passions." After that James passage, if you are wondering how to ask for the "right" things, look no further than the rest of the Sermon. You might also reference Galatians 5. The Lord has made his ways plain.

Write some petitions that are always aligned with God's will as described in the Sermon (i.e., a petition based on Matthew 5:3–12 or 13–16, or Galatians 5:22-23):

Of course, God knows what we need before we ask Him (Matthew 6:32). If this is true, what is the need for prayer? Calvin teaches that in verses 7-11, Jesus is describing the way God chooses to bestow blessings upon us.

> Christ presents the grace of his Father to those who pray. He tells us, that God is of Himself prepared to listen to us, provided we pray to Him, and that his riches are at our command, provided we ask them...But as Christ here addresses disciples, he merely reminds us in what manner our heavenly Father is pleased to bestow upon us his gifts. Though he gives all things freely to us, yet, in order to exercise our faith, he commands us to pray, that he may grant to our requests those blessings which flow from his undeserved goodness. (Calvin, 1555/1846)

When prayer is in play, we are reminded that we are completely dependent upon God. When we regularly pray, we have a harder time foolishly believing that coincidence or self-sufficiency was the cause of our provision. Like Gideon (Judges 6-7), we need to be reminded often that it is solely the Lord's provision that sustains and protects us, not our own. We are always tempted to amass material "protections" to maintain control over our own fortunes, to try to figure things out for ourselves, but we should rely only on God (Psalm 20:7).

Both the exhortation to pray and the promise that our prayers are heard are dependent upon the goodness of God our Father, described in verses 9-11.

Read the following passages and describe the different ways God displays His goodness:

Matthew 14:13-21	

Psalm 37:4	
Psalm 84:11	
Isaiah 49:15	

Matthew 7:7-11 is certainly not a promise to get whatever we ask for in prayer (remember day one of this week and learning how to let go of control). Instead, it is an admonition to pray in accordance with God's will, revealed to us through Christ, the Spirit, and the Word. For a perfect model of this, read and meditate on Matthew 26:39.

As much as we all want to follow the instructions in this passage, there is a challenge that often assaults our prayer life: we can become discouraged when fervent prayers go unanswered. We may ask whether prayer matters at all. This is another reason Jesus summons us to frequent prayer. By meeting regularly with God, we will be sustained in the hope of His goodness instead of discouraged by the apparent lack of His action. This hope is dependent upon our understanding of the balance between providence and prayer. Terrance Tiessen gives us a great understanding of the balance:

> Although God has determined in his timeless eternity all that would happen in created history, he has planned not only the outcomes but the means by which those outcomes are achieved. God has thus given petitionary prayer an effective role in the outworking of his purposes. There are many things that God does providentially, whether or not anyone asks Him to do them. But there are also things that God has purposed to do precisely as answers to prayer. By this means God involves his followers in the work of establishing God's rule in the world, he fosters their sense of dependence on Him, and he generates a thankful spirit when things happen as believers have prayed that they should. The ministry of intercession for one another within the community of God's people also fosters the fellowship that God wills for them. So prayer does affect the outcome of things in the world, although it does not do so by changing God's mind about what he will do in the situation. (Tiessen, 2000)

Can you think of any personal prayers that seem to fall in the category of what is described by Tiessen?

_____

_____

How does today's study influence your own view of petitionary prayer?

_____

_____

Watch Study With Friends Video Series: The Sermon, Episode 7.4

DAY FIVE

CHOOSE KINDNESS

As verses 7:7-11 on prayer recall 6:5-15, so 7:12 on the Law recalls 5:17-20. When Jesus "sums up the Law and the Prophets" in His "Golden Rule" He is not abolishing the Old Testament explanation of different Laws and observances. However, He is also not simply reducing the Law to this summary statement. Instead, He is helping us to comprehend the Law and to see it in its plainest principles.

Both the over-expansion and the oversimplification of the Law can create issues. When we expand the Law into careful, granular commands, it helps us to adhere to it closely, but can cause a distorted or even obscured view of what the Law exists to do in the first place: show us our need for Jesus. When we try to rely upon our own ability to uphold the Law, we forget that we cannot uphold it with any consistency, and we need to be saved from the consequences of breaking it.

What are some practical examples of how we might make the Law too granular?

_____

_____

On the other hand, when we oversimplify the Law to just "grace," we can be tempted to disregard the demands of discipleship, relying on that grace to bail us out of any choices or behaviors we choose.

What are some practical examples of how we might oversimplify the Law?

_____

_____

Here, Jesus provides the balance. The entire Sermon is a prescription for the Christian life. It works out the Law in the context of Christ and shows us how to be His disciples. If we pay attention to that first word "So," (or "Therefore") we see the connective tissue between 7:12 and the surrounding text. This verse, then, has a conclusion feel to it, summarizing the essence not just of the Law but also of the Sermon. In this way, verses 5:17-20 and 7:12 might be considered bookends. In fact, the first word of 7:12 is the Greek word *panta*, which can be translated to "in everything" or reasonably here "the sum of the matter." Though 7:12 is a short verse, it packs a powerful punch.

John Stott makes a further connection between love and grace in 7:6 and 7:12 saying, "If verse 6 is the exception, verse 12 is the rule...It transforms our actions. If we put ourselves sensitively into the place of others and wish for them what we would wish for ourselves, we would never be mean, always generous; never harsh, always understanding; never cruel, always kind" (Stott, 2020, p. 164).

Matthew 22:34-40 reiterates the Golden Rule. Who is Jesus speaking to in this passage? Do you notice anything different about this passage and 7:12?

The early Christian church prioritized this teaching, as evidenced in the *Didache*, which places this instruction at the very beginning, 1:2-5. Interestingly, it provides the Golden Rule in reverse - instead of teaching us to treat others as we would be treated (positive), *Didache* says "Do nothing to another that you would not have befall yourself" (negative).

What are some ways we treat ourselves well/poorly? Make some connections between this and how we treat others:

Both James and Paul strenuously uphold the practice of the Golden Rule. Read the following passages and make note of any nuances you find in how we practice the Golden Rule:

James 2:8	
Romans 13:9-10	
Galatians 5:14	

If 7:12 recalls the earlier Sermon teaching on the Law, it also certainly recalls the earlier Sermon teaching on loving our enemies (5:43-48), putting all things in the perspective of self-love. This is not narcissistic love, but rather a pointed reminder that as we practice love and grace for others, we must be reminded that we, ourselves, are also image-bearers. Self-care leads to good care of others, and in that context, we all become better humans. When I ask myself, "What would I want in this situation?" I am embracing empathy. We can apply that empathy to relationships at home (parent/child, spouse), in our neighborhood (taking and offering help when needed), and at work (manager/employee).

What are some ways that others are kind to you? Are there any ways you wish you were kinder to yourself?

Watch Study With Friends Video Series: The Sermon, Episode 7.5

WEEK EIGHT

KINGDOM COMMITMENT
(MATTHEW 7:13-29)

¹³*Enter by the narrow gate. For the gate is wide and the way is easy that leads to destruction, and those who enter by it are many.* ¹⁴*For the gate is narrow and the way is hard that leads to life, and those who find it are few.* ¹⁵*Beware of false prophets, who come to you in sheep's clothing but inwardly are ravenous wolves.* ¹⁶*You will recognize them by their fruits. Are grapes gathered from thornbushes, or figs from thistles?* ¹⁷*So, every healthy tree bears good fruit, but the diseased tree bears bad fruit.* ¹⁸*A healthy tree cannot bear bad fruit, nor can a diseased tree bear good fruit.* ¹⁹*Every tree that does not bear good fruit is cut down and thrown into the fire.* ²⁰*Thus you will recognize them by their fruits.* ²¹*Not everyone who says to me, 'Lord, Lord,' will enter the kingdom of heaven, but the one who does the will of my Father who is in heaven.* ²²*On that day many will say to me, 'Lord, Lord, did we not prophesy in your name, and cast out demons in your name, and do many mighty works in your name?'* ²³*And then will I declare to them, 'I never knew you; depart from me, you workers of lawlessness.'* ²⁴*Everyone then who hears these words of mine and does them will be like a wise man who built his house on the rock.* ²⁵*And the rain fell, and the floods came, and the winds blew and beat on that house, but it did not fall, because it had been founded on the rock.* ²⁶*And everyone who hears these words of mine and does not do them will be like a foolish man who built his house on the sand.* ²⁷*And the rain fell, and the floods came, and the winds blew and beat against that house, and it fell, and great was the fall of it.* ²⁸*And when Jesus finished*

these sayings, the crowds were astonished at his teaching, ²⁹for He was teaching them as one who had authority, and not as their scribes.
– Matthew 7:13-29

"When Christ calls a man, he bids Him come and die."
-Dietrich Bonhoeffer (1979/1937)

Matthew 7:13-29 concludes the Sermon with an emphasis on the commitment required from His disciples, starting with examples of how that will look and ending with the "why" of Jesus' authority. Jesus warns His listeners about the danger of false prophets and urges us to choose the narrow path that leads to eternal life. He emphasizes the importance of denying ourselves, taking up our cross, and following Him. He cautions against the easy and comfortable way of the broad path and stresses the importance of producing good fruit in our life. He also stresses the need for obedience to God's will and the danger of simply professing faith without putting it into action. Finally, He concludes by elevating the importance of building our lives on a strong foundation of commitment to Him and His teachings.

Matthew 7:28-29 brings us back to week one of our study, reminding us of the scope and breadth of what Jesus has done in the entire Sermon: taught us, with authority, how and why we strive to be His disciples.

DAY ONE

THE NARROW WAY

Last week we spent a lot of time on the everyday choices we make as Christians and we internalized Jesus' exhortations about the choices that differentiate His disciples. What makes Matthew 7:13-14 jarring is the *starkness* of options. In a culture that promotes relative truth alongside the plurality of all preferences being valid, this call to a singular choice is, again, counter cultural. But the choice we are called to make is not new.

Read Psalm 1. What is the choice being made here?

_____

_____

The two options offered in these verses, destruction or life, recall Deuteronomy 30:19-20a. Read that passage and record the choices presented.

_____

_____

Our choice holds dual accountability: here on earth and in heaven. The descriptions of "life" and "destruction" apply to both our earthly life and what happens at its end. Once again, we find the 'already, not yet' mystery of our spiritual life on display.

How has choosing Christ brought you or someone you know life? How has not choosing Him brought you or someone you know destruction?

_____

_____

The start of the passage shows Jesus calling us to enter His kingdom. This was certainly a main theme in all His preaching while He was on earth.

Read the following passages and note the different ways Jesus teaches us how to enter the kingdom.

Mark 9:47	
Mark 10:15	
Matthew 5:19	

As we enter the kingdom we must do so by the narrow gate. Make no mistake, *Jesus* is the gate (John 10:9), and His teaching is inextricable from His person and work. The call to discipleship is a call to follow Him in relationship and in deed. These things cannot be separated. This requires radical commitment, not casual association. Union with Christ is the wellspring of both blessings *and* discipleship. The gate is narrow because it is not easy.

Read the following passages and note the common theme of discipleship:

Luke 9:23

_____

2 Corinthians 1:5

_____

1 Peter 4:13

In Exodus, the people saw the wonder of God and His mighty work and were devoted (Exodus 20:18-19).

Write out the people's response to the wondrous works of God, found in Exodus 24:3:

But not long after, their hearts wandered and their faith faltered. Again and again, God's people are called by their prophets and leaders to renew their commitment to Him (Joshua, Ezra, Nehemiah, etc.). McKnight (2013) explains the connection:

> So when Jesus climbs the mount of this Sermon, assumes the posture of a teacher and lawgiver, issues forth his kingdom demands in ways that develop what Moses has taught, and then summons his followers to kingdom obedience at the end...we are obligated to see Him taking the posture of the Final Prophet, the Messiah. The Sermon is that serious: this is the Messiah's revelation of God's will. The major difference, of course, is that Jesus connects his teachings to the inauguration of the kingdom" (p. 257)

Return to your notes from week one/day one, comparing Jesus to Moses. How, if at all, has your understanding of those parallels been deepened through your study of the Sermon?

The way is narrow because it requires commitment and sacrifice, and those things don't come naturally to us. Prayerfully meditate over the words of Dietrich Bonhoeffer in his *Cost of Discipleship*:

> To confess and testify to the truth as it is in Jesus, and at the same time to love the enemies of that truth, his enemies and ours, and to love them with the infinite love of Jesus Christ, is indeed a narrow way. To believe the promise of Jesus that his followers shall possess the earth, and at the same time to face our enemies unarmed and defenseless, preferring to incur injustice rather than do wrong ourselves, is indeed a narrow way. To see the weakness and wrong in others, and at the same time refrain from judging them; to deliver the gospel message without casting pearls before swine, is indeed a narrow way.
>
> The way is unutterably hard, and at every moment we are in danger of straying from it. If we regard this way as one we follow in obedience to an external

command, if we are afraid of ourselves all the time, it is indeed an impossible way. But if we behold Jesus Christ going on before step by step, we shall not go astray. (Bonhoeffer, 1979/1937)

Watch Study With Friends Video Series: The Sermon, Episode 8.1

DAY TWO

THE DECEIVERS

With the separation between God's kingdom and the world clearly distinguished in the preceding verses, Jesus quickens our application of that separation. Included (in fact underscored) in the next exhortations of the Sermon is the warning about deception. This warning takes two points of view: the deceivers and the deceived.

The separation of Christ's kingdom from the world is an ongoing process. We must be vigilant in discerning the two. Jesus speaks in Matthew 7:15-20 not as if deceivers might come, but with assurance that they have already come and will increase alongside the increase of the kingdom.

Read Matthew 24:11-14 and note what will "increase" (ESV):

_____

In the context of all you have learned studying the Sermon, how do you now interpret that word?

_____

Read the following passages and describe the different types of people Jesus is warning about.

2 Corinthians 11:13	
2 Peter 2:1	
1 John 2:22	

Jesus is blunt in His description of the deceivers: ravenous wolves. This is a reiteration of the sheep/shepherd metaphor. A good shepherd will be vigilant about his sheep, always on guard

143

against the wolf who comes to destroy them. On the other hand, a hired hand, one who cares only for himself and nothing for the sheep, will flee at the sight of danger and leave the sheep to be devoured.

Read John 10:11-13 and put this imagery into modern terms. What are some examples you can name?

_____

_____

Paul has this same concern for the churches he planted (Acts 20:29-31). It seems from these passages there are wolves prowling around every corner, seeking to devour our faith in Christ. Well, there are, but Jesus has given us the key to their cages.

Read Matthew 7:15-20. What word is repeated? How many times?

_____

Earlier in our study we noted that when something is repeated, we should take note. The redundancy in these verses is hard to ignore. Again and again, Jesus tells us to judge people by what their life and work is producing. Words are easily shined and easily tarnished, but actions that persist over a long period of time are harder to deny.

Can you think of anyone whose words and actions did not align? Take a moment to honestly reflect on when this was true of your own words and actions.

_____

_____

In his parallel passage, James adds an element to the visual. What element does James 3:12 add to Matthew 7:15-20?

_____

Read John 7:37-38. How does Jesus describe Himself?

_____

Since there is clear truth and falsehood in what Jesus is describing, and since He assures us that deceivers will be around us, we are to be cautious.

One thing that has always struck me is that there is no "letter to the Bereans" in the bible. This community of believers is named in the Bible alongside other communities where Paul delivered the gospel and left behind disciples to carry on the building of the Church. I am convinced that there is an example to follow in Berea, and I think it speaks to our study today.

Read Acts 17:10-13 and answer the following:

Were the Bereans Jews or Gentiles?

What is the word used to describe them in comparison to the Thessalonians?

How did they receive the Word?

What did they do to make sure the preaching was true, and how often did they do that?

Calvin reminds, "It is the will of the Lord, (as has been already said,) that his Church shall be engaged in uninterrupted war in this world. That we may continue to be his disciples to the end, it is not enough that we are merely submissive, and allow ourselves to be governed by his Word. Our faith, which is constantly attacked by Satan, must be prepared to resist" (Calvin, 1555/1846).

Jesus will not leave us defenseless. His Word and His Spirit guide us to truth, but we must participate in the pursuit.

Watch Study With Friends Video Series: The Sermon, Episode 8.2

DAY THREE

THE DECEIVED

Matthew: 7:17-20 and 21-23 are linked, so as we begin this day studying the latter portion, let's be mindful of the former.

Write your own summary of Matthew 7:17-20

_____

_____

If Matthew 7:17-20 focuses on discernment by "bearing," Matthew 7:21-23 focuses on discernment by "doing." One is the action, the other is the product of that action. Both should be clearly observable in the life of a true disciple.

Read both sections again and note the number of times the word "bear" or "bears" appears in 17-20, and the number of times you see "does," "did," or "do" in 21-23.

_____

Though we use the ESV for this study, it's noteworthy that the NIV translation of the last word in verse 23 is evil**doers**.

Perhaps it's obvious, but this passage is clearly talking about false *Christians*. They say "Lord, Lord," which means they call Jesus Lord. They prophesy and perform miracles in *His* name.

Read Matthew 24:24 and summarize it:

_____

It seems like these great signs and wonders would be the fruit that Jesus previously described. If you are like me, these passages make you a little anxious, crying out "How, then, will we know??"

Romans 10:9-10 tells us that we must confess with our mouth that Jesus is Lord, but it also says we must believe with our heart. This is the difference between genuine faith and one that is hypocritical. Christianity is not a behavior modification program; it is a transformation of the heart by the person and work of Christ. To attempt to put actions before that transformation is to wrestle our own flesh into temporary obedience, but without the Holy Spirit to sustain us in transformation, we will ultimately (and frequently) fail. Our good deeds will be hollow, our charitable actions will be inconsistent. This is what Jesus is telling us to look for.

Read and rephrase 1 Corinthians 12:3:

_____

_____

The main question is this: Do the prophet's/teacher's/leader's actions complement their profession of faith or compete with it? This necessary observation is woven throughout the Sermon as Jesus points out hypocritical behavior in several instances.

Read Luke 6:46. What is the question?

_____

What are some reasons you can think of that might cause a person to call Jesus "Lord" and not really live a life under His Lordship?

_____

_____

Read 2 Timothy 2:19. What is being asked or required of "those who are His?"

_____

_____

In *The Cost of Discipleship*, Bonhoeffer (1979/1937, p. 194) suggests we can replace the word 'love' in 1 Corinthians 13:1-3 with the name of Christ.

Write that passage, replacing the words accordingly:

If you examine this carefully, you see that it is possible to do many great and "churchy" things without having unity with Christ.

There is a notable lack of instruction in Matthew 7:21-23 about what Christians and the Church are to do about false Christian prophets. This passage does not address church discipline, but verse 23 assures us they will be judged.

Read Matthew 13:36-43. Note similarities and differences from 7:21-23:

Earlier in our study we learned about a man who stapled apples to his apple tree in hopes of impressing those around him with his good works. As we examine the text today, it's worth saying that we can all be tempted to "fake it" sometimes, and that doesn't make us false prophets. It does, however, make us deceivers/deceived in that apple-stapled area of our life. If we have more stapled apples than real ones, it's time to take a hard look at our understanding of the gospel and of grace.

We need to look no further than the Sermon for specific types of fruit. True disciples of Christ care for their neighbors, those in need, and the marginalized. True disciples exhibit grace and love vs. being censorious and harshly judgmental. True disciples teach their children to nurture patience and be peacemakers, and they serve their spouses with humility.

McKnight asserts that this text is primarily aimed at gifted leaders in the church, saying, "it is designed to probe into the life of the charismatically gifted leader in order to get Him or her to realize that gifts are not enough, that the fruit of love in life is what matters most." I would contend that each of us is potentially leading someone, so it applies to us all, but James 3:1 supports McKnight's higher standard for teachers/leaders.

In all cases, the Spirit of God has been given to us for discernment.

Read and reflect on 1 John 2:3-6, 26-27. How can we practically apply the warnings in our life today?

_____

_____

The Spirit of the Lord that lives in us helps us to see and identify the Spirit (or lack thereof) in others. We are not meant to do this on our own, and certainly not meant to do so flippantly.

The life of a Christian leader is a hard one, so be gracious and merciful toward them. But when that Spirit stirs in you and you feel uneasy or uncertain about someone, prayerfully pay attention to that stirring. Patiently wait on the Lord to show you His truth. Thoughtfully decide what to do in response. Honor God in each step of the process, and He will lead you.

Consider Calvin's assessment: "We know what a strong propensity men have to falsehood, so that they not only have a natural desire to be deceived, but each individual appears to be ingenious in deceiving himself" (Calvin, 1555/1846).

Watch Study With Friends Video Series: The Sermon, Episode 8.3

DAY FOUR

HEARING AND DOING

Matthew 7:21-23 is about *saying* and doing, and 7:24-27 is about *hearing* and doing. The message is similar, and that's not surprising. We have seen remarkable consistency throughout the entire Sermon. This passage warns us to pay attention to foundations. Imagine the houses described are exactly the same, and we can't really see the difference in outward appearances. This, again, is instruction about professing Christians: these are the people who hear His words.

Where are some places/circumstances where we hear Jesus' words?

_____

_____

These three last segments of the Sermon emphasize the importance of hearing the truth of what Jesus has taught and doing the things He instructs us to do. They are the perfect conclusion to the Sermon.

During the last two days of study, we learned about deceivers and the deceived. The corresponding James passage sheds light on this instruction to hear and do.

Read James 1:22. What word do you recognize? What is the deepening of the message that this phrase provides?

_____

_____

Read the entirety of James 1:19-27 and make notes about the practical applications James spells out when he speaks of hearing and doing.

_____

_____

What are some ways you find yourself experiencing a disconnect between hearing and doing God's word?

_____

_____

I will confess that I must make a regular practice of emotional "doing." As a teacher (and student) of the Bible, my first instinct is to grasp the precepts with my brain, not my heart. I must intentionally remind myself that God's Word is not just for me to learn about, but its purpose is the transformation of my life, starting with my heart. I like how Luke phrases the wise man's foundation as being "dug deep" (6:48). We really must let the truth of our sin and the gospel of forgiveness do its work down deep. Of course, intellectual pursuit of God honors Him. But head knowledge alone is no substitute for practical, daily obedience.

This is a good time to remind ourselves we do not have a salvation of works, supported by all this talk of "doing." Rather, we believe that 1 John 1:6 (If we say we have fellowship with Him while we walk in darkness, we lie and do not practice the truth) and 1 John 2:4 2:4 (Whoever says "I know Him" but does not keep His commandments is a liar, and the truth is not in Him) are expressions of the perfect marriage between our faith and our actions. Faith always comes first.

Read Hebrews 11:6 and rephrase the importance of faith:

_____

Where the previous passages taught us that the discernment between true and false disciples comes from their fruit or from their actions, here, the discernment comes during the storm. Where do we turn in the storm? The storm reveals the truth. This storm can be understood as the trials of life (Psalm 69:2) or as the final judgment (Genesis 6-7, Proverbs 10:25, etc.). The cataclysm in both cases is separation from Jesus.

Read the following passages and write the description of God from each:

Nahum 1:7

_____

Isaiah 25:4-5

_____

Psalm 55:6–8

One evening, when my youngest daughter was about 4 or 5, she was in her room when the power went out in our whole neighborhood. Her room was plunged into darkness. I happened to be in my bedroom, right across the hall, watching TV in bed with the hubby. Moments after the power went out, I heard her cry out, "Mommy, I'm in a dark room and I can't find you!!" She was paralyzed with fear, and all she could think of was to cry out to me because she trusted me to know how to get her through the problem.

This is a perfect example of how true disciples respond in the storm. One of my favorite local radio pastors, Rev. Wayne Monbleau, says we should "Make a well-worn path into the presence of Jesus so that in a time of darkness we can find our way."

Do you know what I did when my baby girl cried out for me? I jumped out of bed and ran to her. On my way I called, "I'm coming!" I often think of this as how God runs to us when we cry out to Him during a storm. How much more than an earthly mom can we trust and have faith in our heavenly Father?

So, the Sermon ends in harmony with its message throughout: Do not be like them. Build your foundation on something better than the world has to offer. Build your life on Christ.

Watch Study With Friends Video Series: The Sermon, Episode 8.4

DAY FIVE

TRUST HIS AUTHORITY

How do we summarize the message of the Sermon? For sure, the main theme is counter-cultural Christianity, encapsulated in the phrase "Do not be like them." Jesus is so patient and merciful in this all-important Sermon. He provides us with examples, warnings, parables, and metaphors so we can really grasp what He is saying. This teaching is as relevant and real today as it was when He first taught it.

But He is also stern in His requirement of obedience and love for the Law. "Jesus does not set before His followers a string of easy ethical rules, so much as a set of values and ideals which is entirely distinct from the way of the world" (Stott, 2020, p. 180). He provides us with the strength and ability to do all of this through His Spirit. The Sermon is Christ's kingdom vision for His kingdom people.

Write out, word for word, 1 Thessalonians 5:23-24, capitalizing all of verse 24:

_____

_____

_____

Summarize your most meaningful notes from each week. Imagine you had to recap the main message from each section for a friend:

Week One: Introduction to the Sermon

_____

_____

Week Two: Matthew 5:3-12

Week Three: Matthew 5:13-16

Week Four: Matthew 5:17-20

Week Five: Matthew 5:21-48

Week Six: Matthew 6:1-24

Week Seven: Matthew 6:25-7:12

Week Eight: Matthew 7:13-29

Matthew 7:28-29 begs the question: Who is this preacher?

The crowds were amazed at His teaching. This study's focus has been the Sermon's seriousness, how seriously Jesus takes discipleship, and the high expectations He has for His followers. But we don't hear the crowds objecting, saying this is all too hard to do. No, we hear that they were amazed by Him. This is the perfect posture in response to the Sermon. He had opened the scriptures and the Law and shed new light on them. ***He taught as one who had authority, and not as their teachers of the Law.***

John Stott summarizes it this way: "He was a Jew, but his message was not Jewish. He was interpreting Moses' law, but in such a way as to show that it was God's. What He had to say was not culturally conditioned in the sense that it was limited to a particular people (Jews) or a particular place (Palestine). Being absolute, it was universal" (Stott, 2020, p. 183).

Jesus does not say 'Thus says the Lord" like other prophets or teachers. Instead, he says 'Truly I tell you" or "But I tell you" because He does not just have authority, He *is* the authority. He is our prophet, priest, and king.

The theme of the Book of 1 John is "Trust and Obey." This is an important theme at the end of the Sermon. I commend your study of 1 John next, as you attempt to put into practice everything taught here in the Sermon. We must always remember that He who teaches us is worthy of our trust and obedience. Fall afresh into the cycle of hearing and doing: trusting Him, obeying Him, seeing that obedience brings the fruit of His promises, and allowing that to cause you to trust Him even more.

We have leaned heavily on three authors as we studied, John Stott, Scot McKnight, and Dietrich Bonhoeffer. It is Bonhoeffer who deserves the last word.

> We have listened to the Sermon on the Mount and perhaps have understood it. But who has heard it aright? Jesus gives the answer at the end. He does not allow his hearers to go away and make of his sayings what they will, picking and choosing from them whatever they find helpful, and testing them to see if they work. He does not give them free rein to misuse his word with their mercenary hands, but gives it to them on condition that it retains exclusive power over them. Humanly speaking, we could understand and interpret the Sermon on the Mount in a thousand different ways. Jesus knows only one possibility: simple surrender and obedience, not interpreting it or applying it,

but doing and obeying it. That is the only way to hear his word. But again he does not mean that it is to be discussed as an ideal, he really means us to ***get on with it*** [emphasis added]. (Bonhoeffer, 1979/1937, p. 197)

Watch Study With Friends Video Series: The Sermon, Episode 8.5

REFERENCES

Bavinck, H. (1909). *The Philosophy of Revelation*. Longmans, Green, and Co.

Bonhoeffer, D. (1955). *Ethics* (E. Bethge, Ed. & N. H. Smith, Trans.). Macmillan Publishing Co., Inc. (Original work published 1949)

Bonhoeffer, D. (1979). *The Cost of Discipleship* (R. H. Fuller, Trans.). Macmillan Publishing Co., Inc. (Original work published 1937)

Calvin, J. (1846). *Commentary on a Harmony of the Evangelists, Matthew, Mark, and Luke* (W. Pringle Trans.). The Edinburgh Printing Company. (Original work published 1555)

Doriani, D. M. (2006). *The Sermon on the Mount: The Character of a Disciple*. P & R Publishing.

Kessler, R. C., Berglund, P. A., Demler, O., Jin, R., Merikangas, K. R., & Walters, E. E. (2005). Lifetime prevalence and age-of-onset distributions of DSM-IV disorders in the National Comorbidity Survey Replication. *Archives of General Psychiatry, 62*(6), 593-602.

Lazzaro, H. (2021, June 26). *Understanding the Old Testament*. Study With Friends. https://studywithfriends.org/wp-content/uploads/2021/07/A-Covenant-Understanding-of-the-Old-Testament.pdf

Lewis, C. S. (1949). *The Weight of Glory and Other Addresses*. Macmillan Publishing Co., Inc.

Ligon, E. M. (1935). *The Psychology of Christian Personality*. Macmillan Publishing Co., Inc.

McCartney, D. G. (2009). *James* (R. Yarbrough, Ed.). Baker Publishing Group.

McKnight, S. (2013). *Sermon on the Mount* (T. Longman, Ed.) Zondervan.

Nesch, E. (Ed.). (2018). *Early Christian Commentary of the Sermon on the Mount*. Elliot Nesch, 2nd edition.

Pelikan, J. (1988). *The Melody of Theology*. Cambridge: Harvard University Press.

Spurgeon, C. (1889) *The Salt-Cellars: Being a Collection of Proverbs, Together With Homely Notes Thereon*. A.C. Armstrong and Son.

Stott, J. (1987). *The Message of the Sermon on the Mount*. InterVarsity Press.

Tiessen, T. L. (2000). *Providence & Prayer: How does God work in the World?*. InterVarsity Press.

Veenhof, J. (2006) *Nature and Grace in Herman Bavinck: Translated by Albert M. Wolters*. Dordt College Press.

Appendix A

Parallels between the Sermon on the Mount and the Book of James

Following is a list of some parallels between the book of James and the Sermon on the Mount:

God's heart for the poor in the kingdom.

"Blessed are the poor in spirit, for theirs is the kingdom of heaven…Blessed are the meek, for they shall inherit the earth." (Matthew 5:3, 5)

"Listen, my beloved brothers, has not God chosen those who are poor in the world to be rich in faith and heirs of the kingdom, which He has promised to those who love Him?" (James 2:5)

Blessed are the mourners.

"Blessed are those who mourn, for they shall be comforted." (Matthew 5:4)

"Be wretched and mourn and weep. Let your laughter be turned to mourning and your joy to gloom. Humble yourselves before the Lord, and He will exalt you." (James 4:9-10)

Mercy to the merciful.

"Blessed are the merciful, for they shall receive mercy." (Matthew 5:7)

". . . judgment is without mercy to one who has shown no mercy. Mercy triumphs over judgment." (James 2:13)

Blessed are the peacemakers.

"Blessed are the peacemakers, for they shall be called sons of God." (Matthew 5:9)

"And a harvest of righteousness is sown in peace by those who make peace." (James 3:18)

Rejoice and be glad in your trials.

"Blessed are those who are persecuted for righteousness' sake, for theirs is the kingdom of heaven. Blessed are you when others revile you and persecute you and utter all kinds of evil against you falsely on my account. Rejoice and be glad, for your reward is great in heaven, for so they persecuted the prophets who were before you." (Matthew 5:10-12)

"Count it all joy, my brothers, when you meet trials of various kinds." (James 1:2)

The example of the prophets.

"Rejoice and be glad, for your reward is great in heaven, for so they persecuted the prophets who were before you." (Matthew 5:12)

"As an example of suffering and patience, brothers, take the prophets who spoke in the name of the Lord." (James 5:10)

The necessity of righteousness.

". . . I tell you, unless your righteousness exceeds that of the scribes and Pharisees, you will never enter the kingdom of heaven." (Matthew 5:20)

". . . whoever keeps the whole law but fails in one point has become accountable for all of it." (James 2:10)

Avoid sinful anger before a righteous God.

"But I say to you that everyone who is angry with his brother will be liable to judgment; whoever insults his brother will be liable to the council; and whoever says, 'You fool!' will be liable to the hell of fire." (Matt. 5:22)

". . . the anger of man does not produce the righteousness of God." (James 1:20)

Do not swear oaths.

"Again you have heard that it was said to those of old, 'You shall not swear falsely, but shall perform to the Lord what you have sworn.' But I say to you, Do not take an oath at all, either by heaven, for it is the throne of God, or by the earth, for it is his footstool, or by Jerusalem, for it is the city of the great King. And do not take an oath by your head, for you cannot make one hair white or black. Let what you say be simply 'Yes' or 'No'; anything more than this comes from evil." (Matthew 5:33-37)

"But above all, my brothers, do not swear, either by heaven or by earth or by any other oath, but let your 'yes' be yes and your 'no' be no, so that you may not fall under condemnation." (James 5:12)

Be perfect and complete.

"You therefore must be perfect, as your heavenly Father is perfect." (Matthew 5:48)

"And let steadfastness have its full effect, that you may be perfect and complete, lacking in nothing." (James 1:4)

Do not lay up treasures on earth where moth and rust destroy.

"Do not lay up for yourselves treasures on earth, where moth and rust destroy and where thieves break in and steal." (Matthew 6:19)

"Your riches have rotted and your garments are moth-eaten. Your gold and silver have corroded, and their corrosion will be evidence against you and will eat your flesh like fire. You have laid up treasure in the last days. Behold, the wages of the laborers who mowed your fields, which you kept back by fraud, are crying out against you, and the cries of the harvesters have reached the ears of the Lord of hosts. You have lived on the earth in luxury and in self-indulgence. You have fattened your hearts in a day of slaughter." (James 5:2-5)

You cannot serve God and be friends with the world.

"No one can serve two masters, for either he will hate the one and love the other, or he will be devoted to the one and despise the other. You cannot serve God and money." (Matt. 6:24)

"You adulterous people! Do you not know that friendship with the world is enmity with God? Therefore whoever wishes to be a friend of the world makes Himself an enemy of God." (James 4:4)

God's provision for tomorrow.

"Therefore do not be anxious about tomorrow, for tomorrow will be anxious for itself. Sufficient for the day is its own trouble." (Matthew 6:34)

"Come now, you who say, 'Today or tomorrow we will go into such and such a town and spend a year there and trade and make a profit'—yet you do not know what tomorrow will bring. What is your life? For you are a mist that appears for a little time and then vanishes." (James 4:13-14)

Be slow to judge.

"Judge not, that you be not judged. For with the judgment you pronounce you will be judged, and with the measure you use it will be measured to you. Why do you see the speck that is in your brother's eye, but do not notice the log that is in your own eye? Or how can you say to your brother, 'Let me take the speck out of your eye,' when there is the log in your own eye? You hypocrite, first take the log out of your own eye, and then you will see clearly to take the speck out of your brother's eye." (Matthew 7:1-5)

"Do not speak evil against one another, brothers. The one who speaks against a brother or judges his brother, speaks evil against the law and judges the law. But if you judge the law, you are not a doer of the law but a judge. There is only one lawgiver and judge, he who is able to save and to destroy. But who are you to judge your neighbor?" (James 4:11-12)

Ask and receive.

"Ask, and it will be given to you; seek, and you will find; knock, and it will be opened to you. For everyone who asks receives, and the one who seeks finds, and to the one who knocks it will be opened." (Matthew 7:7-8)

"You desire and do not have, so you murder. You covet and cannot obtain, so you fight and quarrel. You do not have, because you do not ask. You ask and do not receive, because you ask wrongly, to spend it on your passions." (James 4:2-3)

Ask your good and wise God, who loves to give good things.

"Ask, and it will be given to you; seek, and you will find; knock, and it will be opened to you. For everyone who asks receives, and the one who seeks finds, and to the one who knocks it will be opened. Or which one of you, if his son asks him for bread, will give him a stone? Or if he asks for a fish, will give him a serpent? If you then, who are evil, know how to give good gifts to your children, how much more will your Father who is in heaven give good things to those who ask Him!" (Matthew 7:7-11)

"If any of you lacks wisdom, let Him ask God, who gives generously to all without reproach, and it will be given him. . . . Every good gift and every perfect gift is from above, coming down from the Father of lights with whom there is no variation or shadow due to change." (James 1:5, 17)

Recognize them by their fruits.

"You will recognize them by their fruits. Are grapes gathered from thornbushes, or figs from thistles?" (Matthew 7:16)

"Can a fig tree, my brothers, bear olives, or a grapevine produce figs? Neither can a salt pond yield fresh water." (James 3:12)

Be doers, not just hearers, of the word.

"Everyone then who hears these words of mine and does them will be like a wise man who built his house on the rock. And the rain fell, and the floods came, and the winds blew and beat on that house, but it did not fall, because it had been founded on the rock. And everyone who hears these words of mine and does not do them will be like a foolish man who built his house on the sand. And the rain fell, and the floods came, and the winds blew and beat against that house, and it fell, and great was the fall of it." (Matt. 7:24-27)

". . . be doers of the word, and not hearers only, deceiving yourselves." (James 1:22)

APPENDIX B

RECOMMENDED READING

Resources for Marital Issues and Biblical Divorce:

Instone-Brewer, D. (2002). *Divorce and Remarriage in the Bible: The Social and Literary Context*. Eerdmans.

Murray, J. (1961). *Divorce*. P&R Publishing.

Eating Disorder and Body Dysmorphia Resources:

Davis Nelson, H. (2016). *Unashamed*. Crossway.

Eberly, M.C.; Edward, A.D.J. (2008). *Eating Disorders: A Handbook of Christian Treatment*. Remuda Ranch.

Welch, E.T. (2020). *Eating Disorders: The Quest for Thinness*. New Growth Press.

Brand, P.; Yancey, P. (1997). *Fearfully and Wonderfully: The Marvel of Bearing God's Image*. Zondervan.

Smeades, L. (2009). *Shame and Grace: Healing the Shame We Don't Deserve*. HarperOne.

Wilson, E. (1998). *How To Stop Being Your Own Worst Enemy*. Intervarsity Press.

Disability Theology:

DeYoung, T. (2022). Editorial: A Needed Change Is Emerging. *Reformed World*, 70 (1), 2-5.

Cooreman-Guittin, T. (2022). Disability Questions About Embodiment Resurrection. *Reformed World*, 70 (1), 6-11.

Thompson, C.A. (2022). Beyond Curing: Healing as Wholeness. *Reformed World*, 70 (1), 12-18.

Wollrad, E. (2022). How to Turn a Black Man Into a Child in One Second: Gender and Disability. *Reformed World*, 70 (1), 19-25

Leow, W.P. (2022). Perspectives On Disability and Theology from Confucian Societies Asia. *Reformed World*, 70 (1), 26-33.

Duckworth, J., Huinink, C. (2022). Ableism in the Church: "Father Forgive Them for They Know Not What [Or What it is] They Do." *Reformed World*, 70 (1), 34-41.

Cowans, G. (2022). Reformation Messages to The Church: Voices of Disability in a Pandemic. *Reformed World*, 70 (1), 42-47.

Van Ommen, A. L. (2022). When Community Gets in the Way: Reflections on Autism and Worship. *Reformed World*, 70 (1), 48-54

Ng, J., Ho, J., Leow, W.P. (2022). Disability Ministry in Singapore: Current State and Future Prospects. *Reformed World*, 70 (1), 55-61.

Harris, D. (2022). Creating Space for Vocation - Epistle to the Postmodern Church. *Reformed World*, 70 (1), 62-66

Okola, A. (2022). Disability and the Ecumenical Movement. *Reformed World*, 70 (1), 67-72.

George, S. (2022). Disability and Theological Education: A Personal Journey. *Reformed World*, 70 (1), 73-77.